# Places To Be

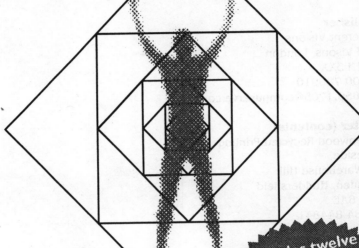

Includes twelve venues in Ireland, Italy, France, Greece, Spain and Turkey!

# 97/98

## A compendium of transformational holidays and places to "just be"

Edited by Jonathan How

**Places to Be 97/98**
A compendium of transformational holidays and places to "just be"

**ISBN**
0 9524396 1 1

© Coherent Visions 1996

**Editor and Designer**
Jonathan How

**Publisher**
Coherent Visions
BCM Visons, London
WC1N 3XX
07000 780910
101650.1705@compuserve.com

**Printer (contents)**
Greenwood Recycled Printing
Lakeside
off Warehouse Hill
Marsden, Huddersfield
HD7 6AE
01484 844841

**Printer (cover)**
Buckingham Colour Press
Riverside Works
Bridge Street
Buckingham
MK18 1EN
01280 824000

**Distributor
(trade and mail order)**
Edge of Time Ltd
BCM Edge, London
WC1N 3XX
07000 780536
106231.456@compuserve.com

# Contents

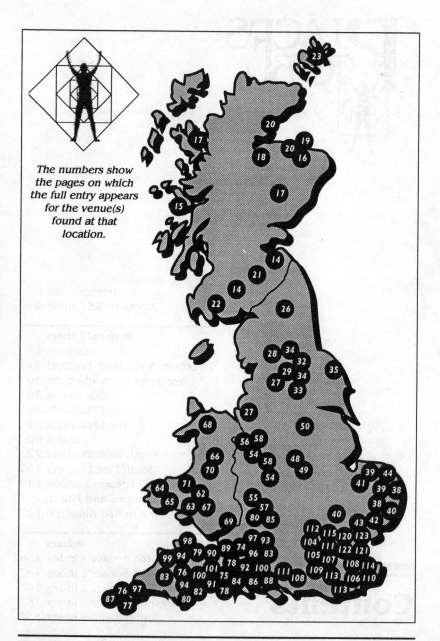

The numbers show the pages on which the full entry appears for the venue(s) found at that location.

Look out for these symbols:

*a member of **Neal's Yard Agency for Personal Development** (see advert pp 10-11). This means that Neal's Yard can supply you with more information about this particular venue. Neal's Yard Agency may carry information about other venues from time to time.*

*also an intentional community and listed in **Diggers and Dreamers - The Guide to Co-operative Living**.*

# Introduction

Welcome to this second edition of *Places to BE*. As time marches relentlessly on towards the new millennium here are a few words from the so-called 'founding father of the New Age':

> *"It was not until the end of the war that I took the vision of using the country house as a potential centre for teaching adults. I thought, 'Why shouldn't we use our country houses, many of which have run into financial difficulty, as cultural centres, not for the upper class, but for all classes?' I knew that what England wanted was the metamorphosis of the weekend house party."*

Sir George Trevelyan, recorded before his death on February 7 1996

Sir George's pioneering work at Attingham Park in Shropshire built a foundation for the movement which is exemplified by the many places listed within this book. The weekend house party has metamorphosed indeed and party-goers of a hundred years ago would scarcely believe their eyes and ears if they saw some of the things which go on in those same country houses today! Not that they would be scandalised. Rather, they would be amazed at the seriousness with which the members of succeeding generations take their own personal growth, education and development.

People are still having fun of course ... but not at the expense

# Introduction

of others. And it's certainly nothing like huntin', shootin' and fishin'!

This book is an introduction to, what for many is, a new world of self-exploratory workshops, retreats and alternative holidays. These events don't just take place in English country houses - there are plenty of venues in Scotland and Wales as well ... and not all locations are grand either. Increasingly, also, there are destinations in places further afield and far away from the British Standard Overcast Sky!

If you bought the first edition of this book then thank you for coming aboard again. The feedback I received was very useful and I've tried to respond to the two most frequent requests in the following ways:

◆ You asked for more information on the types of courses on offer and as a result I've extracted a lot more information from venues on what exactly their specialities are. These appear by their entry and (as far as possible) are tabulated in the various indexes at the back.

◆ You asked for more B&Bs with a difference. There are 65 new entries in this edition and a fair number of these are B&Bs which are either exclusively vegetarian; offer some kind of therapy; or offer a supportive environment for a retreat. It has not always been easy to persuade the typical vegetarian B&B that this book is an appropriate place in which to be listed so I would appreciate your support over the next couple of years in making your favourite B&Bs aware that you use this publication and that you would recommend them having an entry in it.

I hope that you will find all the new information to be useful. Inevitably there will be inconsistencies due to different interpretation by the people who filled out the forms. It's at this point that I should probably emphasise that I have not vetted the places in this book. I'm moving towards a process of at least visiting them all but it will be a long time before I set off with my clipboard and don an AA style inspector's cap! If you have a negative experience of a venue I would suggest that you first raise it with the place concerned and only if you meet a blank wall should you contact me. I am a publisher rather than an ombudsperson so I'm not offering to mediate in disputes! I should also point out that I cannot be held responsible for anything that may occur to individuals visiting the venues in this directory.

Phew! Well now we've got that out of the way I'll get on to the much more interesting area of how to use the directory ...

The bulk of the book is made up of regional sections containing the detailed description of each venue. If you're just idly browsing then this is the place to do it! Within the regions places are simply listed alphabetically - I tried putting them in the order of a logical tour in the first edition but everybody else's logic seemed different to mine! The numbers on both the England, Scotland & Wales map (page 4); the regional maps; and the various indexes; refer to the page on which the venue is described - there is no venue numbering system.

In addition to the basic contact details and description each place may or may not have entries under:
*SPIRITUAL ORIENTATION*
*ACCOMMODATION*
various, mostly self-explanatory, features
*EVENT TYPES*
different types of retreats, courses etc
*SUITABILITY OR SPECIALISM*
courses aimed at or premises suited to a particular group
*SUBJECT SPECIALITIES*
very broad subject areas.

The B&Bs listed in *Places to BE* are all distinctive in some way, even if that way is simply that they offer vegetarian food. The list does not, however, claim to be comprehensive in any way (for instance there are a number of very good vegetarian B&B guides already, containing hundreds of addresses, and it would be pointless to replicate them).

Many of those in *Places to BE* are representative of a new breed of B&B which offer something more than just food and accommodation. Perhaps it is some kind of educational service, perhaps a healing therapy. Turn to the **B&B Seeker's Index** on page 138 for the fast track to finding a bed and breakfast place.

People from all religions have been going on retreats for hundreds, if not thousands, of years. As the pace of life in the industrialised world speeds up this ancient form of getting away from it all has suddenly started to rise in popularity again and, notably, amongst people who do not see themselves as attached to a particular religion.

Many Christian establishments cater for this demand, often on quite a large scale. There are also, however, a growing number of smaller venues offering retreats. You need to check whether the retreats are for individuals or groups; whether they are based on any particular spiritual system; how much guidance is available and/or how much you will be left to your own devices. **The Retreat Seeker's Index** on page 143 is there to help you get started on this route.

## Introduction

If you run courses or workshops yourself then you'll be wanting **The Venue Seeker's Index** (page 148).

You'll probably find it easiest to start with the approximate numbers. The information in *Places to BE* is meant to be a starting point, so there is no detail on numbers of twin/ triplet/ quadruplet rooms etc. However, you will be able to get a rough idea from the ratio of bedspaces to rooms. Contact the venue for more details.

The index also contains a number of other accommodation features relevant to making a choice on hiring. There is also minimal information on pricing.

If you're keen to participate in workshops and courses then head for **The Workshop Seeker's Index** on page 155.

Here you will find a matrix showing venues (in regional groups) against subject speciality headings as follows:

**S1** Arts & Crafts
drawing; painting; pottery; etc
**S2** Self expression
music; writing; drama, etc
**S3** Bodywork & Breathwork
massage; bio-energetics; breathwork; rebirthing; etc
**S4** Health & Healing
acupressure; aromatherapy; homeopathy; psychic healing; etc
**S5** Outdoor activities & Sport
walking; climbing; inner sport; etc

**S6** Conservation work
woodland work; hedge laying; etc
**S7** Food & Horticulture
diet modification; cookery; organic gardening; permaculture;
**S8** Altve. lifestyles & technology
communal living; technology; etc
**S9** Counselling
spiritual; psychotherapeutic; individuals; couples; etc
**S10** Inner process
dreamwork; gestalt; hypnosis; regression; etc
**S11** Group process
teamwork; trust building; psychodrama; etc
**S12** Ritual & Shamanic
vision quest; ancient wisdom; ceremony; etc
**S13** Earth mysteries
ancient sites; geomancy; etc
**S14** Meditation
guided visualisation; attunement; inner listening; concentration; etc
**S15** Prayer
contemplative; devotional; chanting; mantras; etc
Of course, the above can only be a very crude guide and you should contact each venue for more detailed information.

So here it is. I hope that you will find the book (and particularly all the new cross-indexes) useful. Thanks to all those places that have contributed entries; to Ulrike, Emily and William for all their follow-up phone calls; and Chris and Medusa for their scrupulous proof-reading!

# PLACES TO BE

## ... ON LINE ...

Those of you who use a computer and have access to the Internet will be pleased to know that there is now a **Places to BE** world wide web site at:

## http://ourworld.compuserve.com/home pages/coherentvisions/PLACESTB.HTM

It has started fairly basically and will grow from there. Initially names and approximate locations have been listed region by region but you still have to buy the book to get the full addresses! However, as the different venues gradually get their own web sites then links will be installed and electronic mail addresses listed.

If you visit or make use of the site please e-mail me on

## 101650.1705@compuserve.com

as I need to get an idea of how useful it is to people and how the site could be improved.

Who knows - the whole publication might gravitate into a wholly electronic form in years to come ...

## *The only promotions specialists in the field*

★ Established for over 5 years

★ Informs public & media about you and your work

★ Effective promotional packages tailor made to suit your needs

★ Results are often better than other forms of advertising

★ **Neal's Yard Meeting Rooms**: Simple, elegant purposebuilt rooms in the heart of London. The perfect venue for open days to show your photos, slides or video. Excellent value for money.

★ **The Events Guide** reaches 5,500 interested people on our constantly updated mailing list. With a print run of 12,000, having an editorial feature, listing or mail-inserts is very effective.

★ **Neal's Yard 'Taster' workshops** are a popular way of giving a 'sample' of your work to potential clients.

**For a copy of our price list or for more details**
contact Ulrike Speyer or Emily Hynes on Tel/Fax 0171 379 0141
14 Neal's Yard • Covent Garden • London WC2H 9DP

If you are seeking, then you will find . . .
. . . at the only *Travel Agent for Inner Journeys*

To receive your FREE copy of our bimonthly Events Guide
containing the most up to date information on:

workshops

training courses

holidays

weekends away

retreats

in the Personal Development field in Britain & abroad

call 0171 379 0141

Drop-in introductory *Taster* workshops

held every Tuesday at 7pm

at Neal's Yard Meeting Rooms

Yoga, Tai Ji, Meditation, Massage, Qi Gong, Healing, Dance, Shamanism, Drumming, NLP,

Chanting, Reiki, Crystals, Dreamwork, Past Lives, Astrology, Aura Soma Colour Therapy,

Feng Shui, Shiatsu, Counselling, Self Hypnosis, Self-Esteem, Swim with Dolphins & more!!

**Neal's Yard Agency for Personal Development**
14 Neal's Yard • Covent Garden • London WC2H 9DP

*K*entigern was the (apparently miraculously conceived) son of Thaney, the daughter of Lothian, a British King in the 6th Century. He later became a student of St Servanus who renamed him Mungo (which meant "dear friend"). Servanus's other disciples were jealous of Mungo, and made a lot of trouble for him. Once, when a robin belonging to St Servanus was accidentally killed, the other boys blamed Mungo. But Mungo took the bird in his hands and prayed, whereupon life returned to it. Glasgow's coat-of-arms still includes a robin in memory of this story of Mungo - who later became its patron saint.

# Scotland

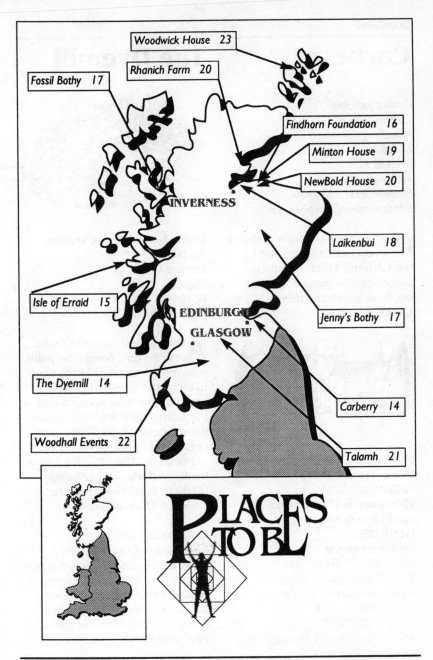

Woodwick House   23

Rhanich Farm   20

Fossil Bothy   17

Findhorn Foundation   16

Minton House   19

NewBold House   20

INVERNESS *

Laikenbui   18

Isle of Erraid   15

EDINBURGH *

GLASGOW *

Jenny's Bothy   17

The Dyemill   14

Carberry   14

Woodhall Events   22

Talamh   21

# PLACES TO BE

# Carberry

# The Dyemill

*Contact: Jock Stein*
*Carberry*
*Musselburgh*
*Midlothian*
*EH21 8PY*
*Telephone: 0131 665 3135*
*Facsimile: 0131 653 2930*
*E-Mail: carberry@dial.pipex.com*

Carberry is a Scottish castle in lovely parkland, owned by the Carberry Trust. A homely place used by people from all over the world. Inclusive Christian ethos.

SPIRITUAL ORIENTATION:
*Christian/Protestant.*
*ACCOMMODATION:*
*90 bedspaces in 40 rooms; Group full board; Venue for hire.*
*EVENT TYPES:*
*Self directed retreats.*
*SUITABILITY OR SPECIALISM:*
*Adults; Children under 12; Couples; Families with children; Men; Women; Young people 12 to 18.*
*SUBJECT SPECIALITIES:*
*Arts & Crafts; Health & Healing; Prayer.*

*Contact: Renate & Charles McMillan*
*The Dyemill*
*Sidmount Avenue*
*Moffat*
*DG10 9BS*
*Telephone: 01683 220681*

A cottage and house to make you "let go". Bring your paint, your music, alone or in company to enjoy the trees in the garden, watch the birds or go for walks in the nearby hills. We offer scrumptious vegetarian B&B (£16 per person) and evening meals (£6 per person). Also ideal for a small family who wish self-catering (£100 to £200 per week). No smoking. Open all year.

*ACCOMMODATION:*
*7 bedspaces in 4 rooms (includes 1 single); Child friendly all ages; Group B&B; Group full board; Group self-catering; Individual B&B; Individual full board; Individual self catering; No smoking in building; Several small spaces; Special diets; Venue for hire.*

# Isle of Erraid

*Contact: Accommodations
Erraid Community, Fionnphort
Isle of Mull
Argyll
PA66 6BN
Telephone: 01681 700384*

A small tidal island off the Ross of Mull near Iona, Erraid has been in the care of the Findhorn Foundation since 1978. The houses (formerly lighthouse keepers' cottages), outbuildings and gardens are home to a small resident group and domestic animals. Our lives and rhythms are very close to the earth, the sea, the tides, the elements and the seasons. Our intention is to consciously embrace Spirit and to live as sustainably as we can, in harmony with nature.

We do not adhere nor exclude any creed or religion and welcome you to the community whatever your previous spiritual involvement. The emphasis is on "living education" and there are great opportunities for learning and growth as you work with us in the garden, kitchen or candle studio, or with maintenance and animals.

Shared accommodation is in single or twin rooms, meals are predominately vegetarian. There is hot and cold water and electricity, but the lavatories are outside earth closets.

SPIRITUAL ORIENTATION:
*New Age.*
ACCOMMODATION:
*20 bedspaces in 14 rooms (includes 7 singles); Child friendly all ages; Group full board; Individual full board; No smoking in building; Special diets.*
EVENT TYPES:
*Own course programme; Working holidays.*
SUITABILITY OR SPECIALISM:
*Adults; Couples; Families with children.*

# Findhorn Foundation

*Cluny Hill College*
*Forres*
*Morayshire*
*IV36 0RD*
*Telephone: 01309 672288*
*Facsimile: 01309 673113*
*E-Mail: reception@findhorn.org*
*World Wide Web: http://www.mcn.org/findhorn/edu/eduindex.html*

An international spiritual community and aspiring eco-village first known for work with nature. Has since become a centre for holistic education and sustainable/ecological living. Extensive workshop programme.

*ACCOMMODATION:*
*Exclusively vegetarian.*
*EVENT TYPES:*
*Own course programme.*
*SUBJECT SPECIALITIES:*
*Alternative lifestyles & technology;*
*Bodywork & Breathwork; Health &*
*Healing; Inner process; Meditation;*
*Self expression.*

# Fossil Bothy

Fossil Bothy
13 Lower Breakish
Isle of Skye
IV42 8QA
Telephone: 01471 822297
Facsimile: 01471 822799

Situated on the seashore in the magical Isle of Skye, with seals, otters and herons for neighbours, giant fossils along the shore, and others in the walls of the building, Fossil Bothy surrounds you with nature and the elements.

A uniquely restored croft, with a special atmosphere which calms the soul - an ideal retreat location, this small and intimate place will help you catch up with yourself and get close to friends. A cosy home from home for a group of eight, with comfortable simple self-catering accommodation and a warm welcome in a special place. £7 per person per night - discounts for groups of eight staying one week or more. Woodstove and all facilities provided.

ACCOMMODATION:
8 bedspaces in 2 rooms; Group self-catering; Venue for hire.

# Jenny's Bothy

Contact: Jenny Smith
Jenny's Bothy, Dellachuper
Corgarff, Strathdon
Aberdeenshire
AB36 8YP
Telephone: 019756 51449

Beautiful unusual self-catering accommodation "where the wild things know no fear"! Paradise for children, occasional venue for workshops, courses. Ideal for its qualities of silence and retreat, the Bothy is situated in an area written up for its standing stones and bird watching. Visit local artists' galleries, ceilidhs, castles and gardens. Balmoral and Lochnagar 17 miles. Cross country or down-hill ski in winter.

The accommodation (in a converted barn) comprises all basic amenities and sleeps up to ten in two rooms. It is heated by a wood-burning stove. Ideal for individuals, families: £7/person/night, children half-price. Group reductions. Space for tents.

*ACCOMMODATION:*
*10 bedspaces in 2 rooms; Camping; Child friendly all ages; Group self-catering; Individual self catering; Several small spaces; Venue for hire.*
*EVENT TYPES:*
*Group retreats; Regeneration programmes; Self directed retreats.*
*SUITABILITY OR SPECIALISM:*
*All.*

# Laikenbui

*Contact: Therese Muskus*
*Laikenbui*
*Granton Road*
*Nairn*
*IV12 5QN*
*Telephone: 01667 454630*

Watch roe deer and osprey among the abundant wildlife on a tranquil croft with a beautiful outlook over a loch amid natural birch woods. We have free range hens, organic garden, sheep and fly fishing. Large warm chalet (quality unbeaten) or residential caravan provide luxury accommodation or try a natural tipi for a new experience. This is an excellent holiday centre (full details in colour brochure) with low rainfall, plentiful sunshine and sandy beaches along

the Moray Firth with its dolphins. Near Loch Ness, Cairngorm mountains, Cawdor Castle, Speyside distilleries. Tipi £10 to £15 nightly. Caravan £88 to £268 weekly. Chalet £100 to £428 weekly.

*ACCOMMODATION:*
*24 bedspaces in 11 rooms ; Group B&B;*
*Individual self catering; Group self catering;*
*Camping; No smoking in building; Child friendly all ages; Wheelchair accessible.*
*SUITABILITY OR SPECIALISM:*
*Adults; Couples; Families with children;*
*Older people.*
*SUBJECT SPECIALITY:*
*Conservation work.*

# Minton House

*Contact: Judith Meynell*
*Minton House, Findhorn*
*Forres*
*Morayshire*
*IV36 0YY*
*Telephone: 01309 690819*
*Facsimile: 01309 691583*
*E-Mail: minton@findhorn.org*

When you walk into Minton House you immediately feel the space. On entering the meditation room the peace surrounds you. And looking out onto Findhorn Bay you sense the solitude and calm of the water. Since 1984 Minton has been developing as a retreat centre honouring all the main spiritual traditions. Our main purpose is to provide an environment which exerts its healing influence on our guests, and to provide a welcoming atmosphere during their stay. Guests mainly come in need of a short period of rest and replenishment, for the solitude of a personal retreat or to join our interfaith programme which includes events on Sufism, Buddhism, Christianity, music, song, dance,

yoga, relationships, and psychological therapy blended with the spiritual. We have something for everyone, please call us to discuss your visit.

*SPIRITUAL ORIENTATION:*
*Sufi.*
*ACCOMMODATION:*
*18 bedspaces in 8 rooms (includes 2 singles); Child friendly all ages; Exclusively vegetarian; Group B&B; Group full board; Individual B&B; Individual full board; Individual self catering; Large indoor space; No smoking in building; Several small spaces; Venue for hire; Wheelchair accessible.*
*EVENT TYPES:*
*Guided group retreats; Own course programme; Self directed retreats.*
*SUITABILITY OR SPECIALISM:*
*Adults; Couples.*
*SUBJECT SPECIALITIES:*
*Bodywork & Breathwork; Health & Healing; Inner process; Meditation; Prayer.*

# NewBold House ✪

Contact: Helmut & Lis
NewBold House
St Leonards Road
Forres
Morayshire
IV36 0RE
Telephone: 01309 672659

NewBold House is a working spiritual community which welcomes guests to join in community life and educational workshops. It offers an integrated experience of living and relating in a different way.

The atmosphere created in this beautiful old mansion house and its seven acres of woodland and gardens provides a caring and nurturing environment for individual self-exploration and growth.

SPIRITUAL ORIENTATION:
New Age.
ACCOMMODATION:
30 bedspaces in 10 rooms (includes 1 single); Exclusively vegetarian; No smoking in building.
EVENT TYPES:
Own course programme.
SUITABILITY OR SPECIALISM:
Adults.

# Rhanich Farm

Contact: Pam Shaw
Rhanich Farm
The Rhanich
Edderton Tain
Ross-shire
IV19 1LG
Telephone: 01862 821265

Fairly isolated organic hill farm with many breeds of sheep, cattle, dairy goats plus hens and dogs; set in beautiful scenery four miles from the sea (Dornoch Firth). We try to live in harmony with nature and all living things. We offer friendly animals, wholesome and tasty (mostly home produced) food and plenty of natural light and space. Two beds in one room. Field for camping. German and some French spoken.

ACCOMMODATION:
2 bedspaces in 1 room; Camping;
Exclusively vegetarian; Individual B&B;
Individual full board; No smoking in
building.
EVENT TYPES:
Working holidays.
SUITABILITY OR SPECIALISM:
Adults; Men; Women; Young people 12
to 18.
SUBJECT SPECIALITIES:
Alternative lifestyles & technology; Food &
Horticulture.

# Talamh

Contact: Ali Begbie
Talamh
Birkhill House
Coalburn
Lanarkshire
ML11 0NJ
Telephone: 01555 820555

Talamh is set in the Lanarkshire
countryside in Scotland. We have
a 16th Century house set in 50
acres of land which is managed
as a species habitat coupled with
fun and education. Our facilities
include bunk room
accommodation, camping and
workshop space for courses. We
cook vegetarian food with fresh
organic vegetables from our own
garden. We also cater for vegan
diets. Talamh is always open to
new ideas and ventures. Talamh
awaits.

ACCOMMODATION:
14 bedspaces in 3 rooms; Camping;
Exclusively vegetarian; Individual B&B;
Large indoor space; Venue for hire.
EVENT TYPES:
Self directed retreats; Working holidays.
SUITABILITY OR SPECIALISM:
All.
SUBJECT SPECIALITIES:
Alternative lifestyles & technology; Arts &
Crafts; Conservation work; Food &
Horticulture; Health & Healing; Meditation;
Outdoor activities & Sport; Ritual &
Shamanic; Self expression; Young people
12 to 18.

# Woodhall Events 🌀

*Laurieston Hall*
*Castle Douglas*
*Dumfries & Galloway*
*DG7 2NB*
*Telephone: 01644 450633*
*Facsimile: 01644 450633*

From April to September members of this community host residential courses and events, some with visiting workshop leaders: theatre, music, dance, t'ai chi, healing, therapy; lesbian and gay weeks; family holidays. Delicious vegetarian food is provided by Green Cupboards Ltd, a separate workers' co-operative.

Accommodation is mostly in shared bedrooms and there are camping areas for those wanting more privacy. Costs are kept low by visitors helping with domestic chores. We take care of a huge, walled, kitchen garden, and over 100 acres of forest and pasture where you're welcome to wander. There are burnside walks, a loch to swim in and a wood-fired sauna.

Some weeks are adult-only and on others a children's club (minimum age: two years) runs concurrently with workshops. Write for annual newsletter.

*ACCOMMODATION:*
*67 bedspaces in 11 rooms; Camping; Child friendly all ages; Exclusively vegetarian; Group full board; Large indoor space; Special diets; Venue for hire; Wheelchair accessible.*
*EVENT TYPES:*
*Own course programme.*

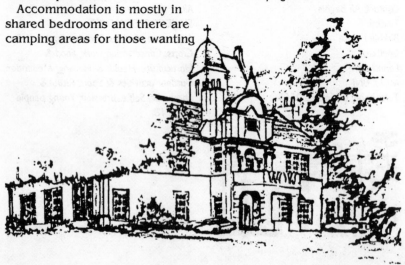

# Woodwick House

Contact: Ann Herdman
Woodwick House
Evie
Orkney
KW17 2PQ
Telephone: 01856 751330
Facsimile: 01856 751383

Set in beautiful archipeligeo, own bay, seal watching, birds and woodland. Peace, good food, ancient sites. In Good Hotel Guide 1996.

ACCOMMODATION:
18 bedspaces in 9 rooms (includes 9 singles); Child friendly all ages; Group B&B; Group full board; Individual B&B; Individual full board; Large indoor space; Special diets; Venue for hire; Wheelchair accessible.
EVENT TYPES:
Own course programme.

---

Joining WWOOF opens up a whole new world of opportunities as well as places where you can find out about different ways of being and doing.

WWOOF is an exchange. In return for work on organic farms, gardens and smallholdings (full time and quite hard!) "WWOOF-ers" receive meals, accommodation and, if necessary, transport to and from the local station.

# WWOOF
## Working for Organic Growers

**Aims**

- to get first hand experience of organic farming and growing
- to get into the countryside
- to help the organic movement which is labour intensive and does not rely on artificial fertilizers for fertility or persistent poisons for pest control
- to make contact with other people in the organic movement

For further information write to WWOOF at 19 Bradford Road, Lewes, East Sussex BN7 1RB

*B*ega was an Irish princess who was shipwrecked off the coast of Cumbria. The Lord of Egremont took her in and she asked him for land to build a nunnery. It was Midsummer's Eve and he jokingly said that she could have every part of his estate that was covered with snow on the next day. Much to his amazement he woke the next morning to find that all the land within three miles of the castle was deep in snow. He kept his word, however, and helped Bega (who later became St Bega or St Bee) to build her nunnery.

# North and North West England

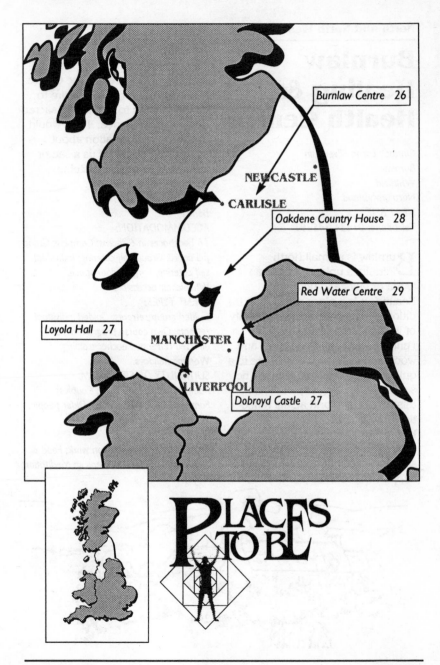

Burnlaw Centre 26

NEWCASTLE

CARLISLE

Oakdene Country House 28

Red Water Centre 29

Loyola Hall 27

MANCHESTER

LIVERPOOL

Dobroyd Castle 27

PLACES TO BE

# Burnlaw Healing & Health Centre

*Contact: Lorna Silverstein*
*Burnlaw*
*Whitfield*
*Northumberland*
*NE47 8HF*
*Telephone: 01434 345391*

Burnlaw is a small North Pennines upland farm in an "Area of Outstanding Natural Beauty". It is a place with a long tradition of occupation and continuity of life style. Standing stones, Pennine walks, winding lanes and woodland valleys all contribute to a quiet beauty. While all life may be seen as a learning experience, in this very busy world actual reflective time is in short supply. The healing and retreat centre aims to create the context for reflective space. All activities allowing this to happen are seen as positive, be it hill walking, painting, dancing, singing, silence, working the land, or study of Holy Texts. The Centre is an expression of our desire to enable people to realise the sacredness of all existence. If you would like further information about Burnlaw please send us a sae or telephone Lorna Silverstein.

*SPIRITUAL ORIENTATION:*
*Baha'i*
*ACCOMMODATION:*
*16 bedspaces in 6 rooms; Camping; Group full board; Group self-catering; Individual self catering; Large indoor space; Wheelchair accessible.*
*EVENT TYPES:*
*Guided group retreats; Guided individual retreats; Own course programme; Self directed retreats; Teacher training; Working holidays.*
*SUITABILITY OR SPECIALISM:*
*Adults; Children under 12; Couples; Families with children; Men; Older people; Women; Young people 12 to 18.*
*SUBJECT SPECIALITIES:*
*Arts & Crafts; Conservation work; Food & Horticulture; Health & Healing; Meditation; Prayer.*

# Dobroyd Castle

*Dobroyd Castle*
*Pexwood Road*
*Todmorden*
*Lancashire*
*OL14 7JJ*
*Telephone: 01706 812247*
*Facsimile: 01706 812247*

L osang Dragpa Centre is a
Buddhist college and retreat
centre based at Dobroyd Castle.
Set on the hillside above the
small Pennine town of
Todmorden it overlooks the
beautiful Calder Valley and is in
the heart of the Pennine walking
country. Part of the New
Kadampa Tradition, the Centre is
home to 25 lay and ordained
Buddhists - studying, practising

and teaching Mahayana
Buddhism. We offer meditation
retreats, courses, working holidays or short breaks in this
peaceful environment. Single,
double and dormitary accommodation available. Good vegetarian
food. All are welcome.

*SPIRITUAL ORIENTATION:*
*Buddhist/Tibetan.*
*ACCOMMODATION:*
*25 bedspaces in 16 rooms (includes 12*
*singles); Camping; Exclusively vegetarian;*
*Group B&B; Group full board; Individual*
*B&B; Individual full board; No smoking in*
*building.*
*EVENT TYPES:*
*Guided group retreats; Working holidays.*
*SUBJECT SPECIALITY:*
*Meditation.*

# Loyola Hall

*Contact: Rev David Birchall*
*Loyola Hall*
*Warrington Road*
*Rainhill, Prescot*
*Merseyside*
*L35 6NZ*
*Telephone: 0151 426 4137*
*Facsimile: 0151 431 0115*

L oyola Hall Spirituality Centre is
situated in its own beautiful
grounds, with lounge, chapel,
prayer-rooms, sauna, jacuzzi, aromatherapy, art room, massage,
and conference rooms. The
Centre has an extensive year-

round programme of retreats and courses, offering everything from day and weekend events to a month's silent retreat. We welcome people of any Christian denomination, and all who seek meaning in life. Residential conference facilities for 45 people: up to 100 for a day event. Conveniently situated close to the M62, between Liverpool and Manchester, with public transport to the door. Ask for our free programme or conference brochure.

SPIRITUAL ORIENTATION:
_Christian.
ACCOMMODATION:
50 bedspaces in 47 rooms (includes 45 singles); Group full board; Individual B&B; Individual full board; Large indoor space; Several small spaces; Special diets; Venue for hire; Wheelchair accessible.
EVENT TYPES:
Accredited courses; Guided group retreats; Guided individual retreats; Own course programme; Self directed retreats.
SUITABILITY OR SPECIALISM:
Adults; Gay men; Lesbian women; Men; Older people; Women; Young people 12 to 18.
SUBJECT SPECIALITIES:
Counselling; Inner process; Meditation; Prayer.

# Oakdene Country House

Contact: David Collier or Hilary Dixon
Oakdene Country House
Garsdale Road, Sedbergh
Cumbria
LA10 5JN
Telephone: 01539 620280
Facsimile: 01539 621501
E-Mail: 100346.14@compuserve.com

Your group has exclusive use of this 1880s grand country house in the Yorkshire Dales National Park for a workshop, meeting, training course, retreat or celebration. We are experienced in responding to the indi-

vidual needs of shared interest groups, families, groups of friends or colleagues. Lounges, log fires, books, comfortable en-suite bedrooms, friendly service, fresh, varied and healthy food, using local produce whenever possible - we cater for omnivores, vegetarians, vegans and crypto-carnivores. Plus we run our own programme of workshops - weekends for women, team building, management. Please phone, fax or e-mail for an information pack. Band B for full occupancy of rooms, Band D for single occupancy of rooms.

*ACCOMMODATION:*
*18 bedspaces in 10 rooms (includes 3 singles); Child friendly all ages; Group B&B; Group full board; Large indoor space; No smoking in building; Several small spaces; Special diets; Venue for hire; Wheelchair accessible.*
*EVENT TYPES:*
*Own course programme; Self directed retreats; Teacher training.*
*SUITABILITY OR SPECIALISM:*
*Adults.*

---

# Red Water Centre

*Back Rough Farm*
*Coalclough Road, Todmorden*
*Lancashire*
*OL14 8NU*
*Telephone: 01706 815328*
*Facsimile: 01706 815328*

Surrounded by woods, hills and tumbling waters Red Water offers a stimulating centre from which to enjoy, explore, create and learn within a rural setting. We offer a variety of weekend arts courses but throughout the year our accommodation and workshop facilities are available for hire. Groups can be self catering or be catered for with our excellent, mainly vegetarian food. Brochure available on request.

*ACCOMMODATION:*
*16 bedspaces in 5 rooms; Group B&B; Group full board; Group self-catering; No smoking in building; Venue for hire.*
*EVENT TYPES:*
*Own course programme.*
*SUBJECT SPECIALITY:*
*Arts & Crafts.*

---

*During the 14th Century John of Bridlington was the prior of the town's Augustinian monastery. One day some sailors were caught in a storm off Flamborough Head. Seeing the tower of Bridlington Priory they prayed to John for help. They were amazed when they saw a monk walking towards them across the huge waves. When he reached their boat he put his hand on the prow and pulled it safely to shore.*
*Not surprisingly he later became St John of Bridlington.*

# Yorkshire & Humberside

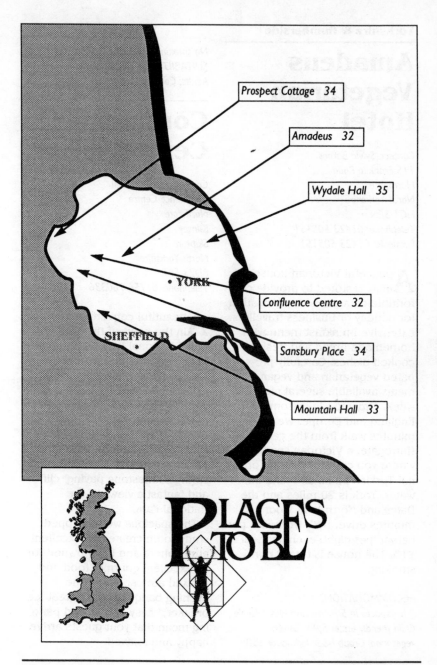

Prospect Cottage  34

Amadeus  32

Wydale Hall  35

• YORK

Confluence Centre  32

SHEFFIELD
•

Sansbury Place  34

Mountain Hall  33

P**LACES**
**TO BE**

# Amadeus Vegetarian Hotel

*Contact: Sylvia Barnes*
*115 Franklin Road*
*Harrogate*
*North Yorkshire*
*HG1 5EN*
*Telephone: 01423 505151*
*Facsimile: 01423 505151*

A peaceful Victorian house lovingly restored to provide comfortable en suite accommodation for holiday or business travellers. Extensive breakfast menu with homemade bread and freshly cooked dishes. Carefully prepared vegetarian and vegan meals available several nights a week. Organic wines from England and Europe. We are ten minutes walk from the centre of Harrogate, a Victorian spa town, where you can still visit the original Turkish baths and take the water. York is 20 miles and the Dales and North York Moors 45 minutes drive. B&B from £21 per person per night; evening meal £13. The house is totally non-smoking.

*ACCOMMODATION:*
*9 bedspaces in 5 rooms (includes 1 single);*
*Child friendly under 5; Exclusively*
*vegetarian; Group B&B; Individual B&B;*
*No smoking in building; Special diets.*
*SUITABILITY OR SPECIALISM:*
*Adults; Couples.*

# Confluence Centre

*Contact: Peter Caswell*
*Confluence Centre*
*Northcote*
*Kilnsey*
*Skipton*
*North Yorkshire*
*BD23 5PT*
*Telephone: 01756 760336*

A beautiful converted barn set in the heart of the Yorkshire Dales National Park, with breathtaking scenery and peaceful surroundings. It is a purpose-built, self-contained course and conference venue with a service tailor-made to your requirements. The Centre is surrounded by 400 acres of private farm land incorporating trout rivers, fresh water springs, limestone paving, cliffs and fantastic views of the National Park.

The spacious well-equipped study room creates an excellent atmosphere and is renowned for its excellent gourmet food and relaxed atmosphere. "The evening banquets are a great ice breaker." Easy access and parking mean that your guests arrive happy and relaxed.

ACCOMMODATION:
*14 bedspaces in 5 rooms; Group B&B; Group full board; Group self-catering; Large indoor space; No smoking in building; Special diets; Venue for hire.*
EVENT TYPES:
*Guided group retreats; Own course programme.*
SUITABILITY OR SPECIALISM:
*Adults; Families with children.*
SUBJECT SPECIALITIES:
*Health & Healing; Outdoor activities & Sport; Self expression.*

# Mountain Hall Centre

Contact: *Mrs S Ledgard*
*Mountain Hall Centre*
*Queensbury*
*West Yorkshire*
*BD13 1LH*
*Telephone: 01274 816258*
*Facsimile: 01274 884001*

Originally designed by a local mill owner as an educational institute for his workers, Mountain Hall, now fully refurbished, is situated at 1200 feet in the Pennines, and conveniently placed for countryside or town. En suite accommodation in single/double rooms; private lounge/bar and restaurant; conference rooms. Acclaimed for quality of menu. Restricted smoking area.

With its inherent tranquil atmosphere, Mountain Hall is available for a 'no hassle' retreat; or as a guided retreat for guests with stress, post-operation trauma, lack of direction or of self-esteem (£280/5 days). Weekend courses on Complementary Therapies and a range of Psychic subjects are offered, £60 including lunches.

ACCOMMODATION:
*22 bedspaces in 13 rooms (includes 4 singles); Group B&B; Venue for hire.*
EVENT TYPES:
*Guided group retreats; Guided individual retreats; Own course programme; Regeneration programmes; Self directed retreats.*
SUITABILITY OR SPECIALISM:
*Adults only.*
SUBJECT SPECIALITIES:
*Earth mysteries; Health & Healing; Inner process; Meditation; Ritual & Shamanic.*

# Prospect Cottage

*Prospect Cottage*
*Bank End*
*Ingleton*
*via Carnforth*
*LA6 3HE*
*Telephone: 015242 41328*

Home-cooked vegetarian/vegan B&B at picturesque Prospect Cottage is only £13/person/night when staying two or more nights. Tranquil, comfortable accommodation ideally situated in the village of Ingleton, on the edge of the Yorkshire Dales National Park and close to Ingleton's famous glens, waterfalls, caves, crags and pot-holes, as well as the village's varied amenities. Visitors travelling by public transport are especially welcome: pick-up from Ribblehead or Bentham BR if required. Accommodation: 3 or 4 bedspaces in one double and one single room, plus bathroom for exclusive use of guests. Own entrance, child friendly, no smoking.

*ACCOMMODATION:*
*4 bedspaces in 2 rooms (includes 1 single); Child friendly all ages; Exclusively vegetarian; Individual B&B; No smoking in building.*

# Sansbury Place Vegetarian Guesthouse

*Contact: Sue Stark*
*Sansbury Place*
*Duke Street*
*Settle*
*North Yorkshire*
*BD24 9AS*
*Telephone: 01729 823840*

We invite you to share our spacious Victorian house with lovely views of the surrounding limestone scenery. We offer an opportunity to unwind and relax in a comfortable, friendly environment and enjoy cosy open fires in the cooler months, or our beautiful garden in the summer.

All food is vegetarian and carefully prepared using a wide variety of fresh and wholefood ingredients (organic where possible). We also offer imaginative vegan and special diet catering. Filtered water is used for drinks and food preparation; environmentally-friendly products are used wherever possible. Settle is a small market town and we are close to the station on the famous Settle to Carlisle railway. Individual B&B £17 to £20; evening meal £10. We regret that we cannot accept dogs.

ACCOMMODATION:
5 bedspaces in 3 rooms (includes 1 single); Child friendly over 5; Exclusively vegetarian; Individual B&B; No smoking in building; Special diets.
SUITABILITY OR SPECIALISM:
Adults; Couples; Gay men; Lesbian women.

# Wydale Hall

Wydale Hall
Wydale Lane
Brompton by Sawdon
Scarborough
North Yorkshire
YO13 9DG
Telephone: 01723 859270
Facsimile: 01723 859702

Wydale, the York Diocesan Centre, is situated within 14 acres of grounds with woodlands. Ideal for retreats, quiet days, conferences, holidays.
Accommodation for 67 guests - groups or individuals. Also self catering accommodation for groups (of 30) in the Emmaus Centre with additional facilities for disabled persons (16) and carers/leaders accommodation (6).

SPIRITUAL ORIENTATION:
Christian/Protestant.
ACCOMMODATION:
67 bedspaces in 34 rooms; Individual B&B; Venue for hire.
EVENT TYPES:
Guided group retreats; Self directed retreats.

St Withburga had founded a nunnery in Norfolk in 654. One year there was a terrible famine and Withburga prayed for help. From nowhere came two milch deer and for the next few days they gave their milk to the nuns. A local huntsman fell from his horse and was killed when he set his dogs on the deer and this was seen as divine punishment. Some years after St Withburga had been buried in the nunnery churchyard her perfectly preserved body was exhumed and taken inside. Her shrine attracted pilgrims for many centuries. The village was named Dereham to commemorate the legend.

# East Anglia

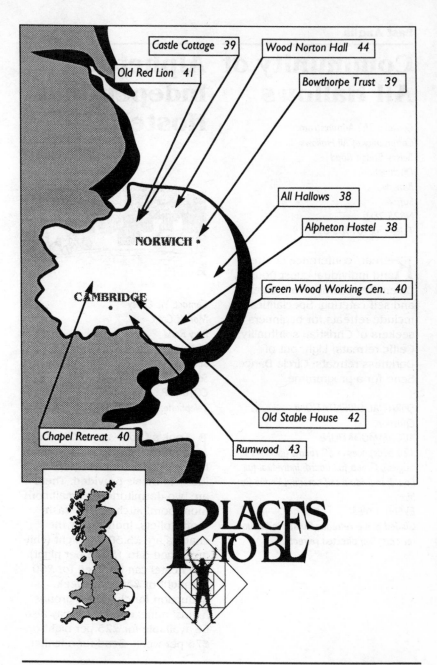

Castle Cottage 39

Old Red Lion 41

Wood Norton Hall 44

Bowthorpe Trust 39

All Hallows 38

Alpheton Hostel 38

Green Wood Working Cen. 40

NORWICH

CAMBRIDGE

Old Stable House 42

Chapel Retreat 40

Rumwood 43

# PLACES TO BE

# Community of All Hallows

*Contact: The Administrator*
*Community of All Hallows*
*Belsey Bridge Road*
*Ditchingham*
*Bungay*
*Suffolk*
*NR25 2DT*
*Telephone: 01986 892749*

Retreat/ conference centres and individual guest houses. Extensive facilities both catered and self catering. Specialities include retreats for beginners or seekers of Christian spirituality; Celtic retreats; Light out of Darkness retreats; Circle Dance. Send for a programme.

*SPIRITUAL ORIENTATION:*
*Christian.*
*ACCOMMODATION:*
*120 bedspaces in 59 rooms (includes 24 singles); Group full board; Individual full board; Individual self catering; Venue for hire.*
*EVENT TYPES:*
*Guided group retreats; Guided individual retreats; Self directed retreats.*

# Alpheton Independent Hostel

*Contact: Vic Copsy*
*Monk's Croft*
*Bury Road*
*Alpheton*
*Sudbury*
*Suffolk*
*CO10 9BP*
*Telephone: 01284 828297*

Monk's Croft - a small hostel offering simple accommodation with basic but adequate facilities. No meals provided. There are two dormitories, a small common room, kitchen and washroom/toilets. Individually the charges are £5.50 per night (children aged 5 to 15: £3 per night). The hostel can be hired for £60 per night or £300 per week. Reduction for children's groups. A girls' annexe (9 beds) may also be available for £25 per night or £75 per week. Send for a leaflet.

ACCOMMODATION:
*20 bedspaces in 3 rooms; Camping; Child friendly over 5; Group self-catering; Individual self catering; No smoking in building; Venue for hire; Wheelchair accessible.*
SUITABILITY OR SPECIALISM:
*Adults; Children under 12; Young people 12 to 18.*

# Bowthorpe Community Trust

*1 St Michael's Cottages
Bowthorpe Hall Road
Bowthorpe Norwich
Norfolk
NR5 9AA
Telephone: 01603 746380*

Saint Michael's Cottage offers short stay accommodation for those seeking rest, renewal or a short break. One single and one double bedroom. Telephone for a brochure.

ACCOMMODATION:
*3 bedspaces in 2 rooms; Individual B&B.*
EVENT TYPES:
*Self directed retreats.*

# Castle Cottage ⛵

*Castle Square
Castle Acre
Norfolk
PE32 2AJ
Telephone: 01760 755888
Facsimile: 01760 755888*

Specialist Macrobiotic B&B and evening meals. Historic rural village setting. Cooking courses; counselling/healing meditation group. Phone for a free brochure. Nigel and Jackie Walker also run "Vegiventures" - see Outside the UK section.

ACCOMMODATION:
*2 bedspaces in 1 room; Exclusively vegetarian; Individual B&B.*
EVENT TYPES:
*Self directed retreats.*

# The Chapel Retreat

*Contact: Sue & Gerry Feakes*
*Church View*
*Chapel Lane*
*Houghton Huntingdon*
*Cambridgeshire*
*PE17 2AY*
*Telephone: 01480 69376/68535*

We offer comfortable modern accommodation, in this riverside village, for groups arranging their own programmes. We have 30 beds in six rooms, lounge, dining room, kitchen, central heating, television/video and table tennis. Children welcome. Brochure available.

ACCOMMODATION:
*30 bedspaces in 6 rooms; Child friendly over 5; Group self-catering; Venue for hire.*

# Green Wood Working Centre

*Contact: Richard King*
*Old Hall*
*East Bergholt*
*Colchester*
*Essex*
*CO7 6TG*
*Telephone: 01206 298294*
*Facsimile: 01206 298996*

A centre for Green Wood Working, specialising in pole lathe wood turning courses from one day to eight days. You can use 3000 year old technology to make a fine frame chair. Also offering courses in making wattle hurdles, hay rakes, "trees to tools" and willow baskets. Location in a community of 60 people living in a converted monastery in 70 acres of Suffolk countryside, making practical steps towards sustainable living by growing much of our own food

organically; sharing fuel, maintenance work and cooking. Simple
accommodation and sharing
community meals can be available to course participants and
working volunteers. Courses from
£20 per day.

*ACCOMMODATION:*
*15 bedspaces in 8 rooms; Camping; Group*
*full board; Individual full board; Venue for*
*hire.*
*EVENT TYPES:*
*Own course programme; Working holidays.*
*SUITABILITY OR SPECIALISM:*
*Adults.*
*SUBJECT SPECIALITIES:*
*Arts & Crafts; Food & Horticulture.*

# Old Red Lion

*Contact: Alison Loughlin*
*The Old Red Lion*
*Bailey Street*
*Castle Acre*
*Norfolk*
*PE32 2AG*
*Telephone: 01760 755557*

Visitors to Castle Acre are
entranced by the special
atmosphere of this mediaeval
walled town. It is now a conservation village with Priory ruins and
Castle earthworks. The Old Red
Lion was once a pub but is now
available for groups to hire (either
with services or on a do-it-yourself
basis - there is a fully equipped
kitchen for self-catering).

Terms are negotiable,
commensurate with the means of
the users and the need for the
enterprise to survive. B&B is also
available on an individual basis.
Exclusively wholefood menus.
Areas for activities include
converted Cellar and Snug. Both
have wood-burners; newly
created Multi-function Space; and
the Courtyard. The Castle
grounds adjoin the property.

*Old Red Lion continued*
*ACCOMMODATION:*
*20 bedspaces in 5 rooms (includes 3*
*singles); Child friendly all ages; Exclusively*
*vegetarian; Group B&B; Group full board;*
*Group self-catering; Individual B&B;*
*Individual full board; Individual self catering;*
*Large indoor space; No smoking in building;*
*Several small spaces; Special diets; Venue*
*for hire.*
*EVENT TYPES:*
*Self directed retreats.*
*SUITABILITY OR SPECIALISM:*
*Adults; Couples; Families with children; Gay*
*men; Lesbian women; Men; Women.*

# Old Stable House Centre

*3 Sussex Lodge*
*Fordham Road*
*Newmarket*
*Suffolk*
*CB8 7AF*
*Telephone: 01638 667190*
*Facsimile: 01638 667190*

This old stable building was converted in 1989 to create a small retreat and spirituality centre with an attractive, restful environment. While conveniently close to the racing town of Newmarket, the house is in a green, secluded setting. The nearby gallops provide lots of scope for walking. The centre supports men and women in their personal and spiritual growth by offering a

programme of workshops and retreats with an holistic, creation-centred focus. In addition, we welcome individuals who are looking for an informal, friendly environment for time out, reflection or retreat on a B&B or self-catering basis. Personal support is available if desired. The facility is available for hire, also on a B&B or self-catering basis; however, catering can be arranged if required.

*ACCOMMODATION:*
*14 bedspaces in 9 rooms (includes 4 singles); Group B&B; Group full board; Group self-catering; Individual B&B; Individual self catering; Large indoor space; No smoking in building; Several small spaces; Special diets; Venue for hire; Wheelchair accessible.*
*EVENT TYPES:*
*Guided group retreats; Guided individual retreats; Own course programme; Self directed retreats.*
*SUITABILITY OR SPECIALISM:*
*Adults.*
*SUBJECT SPECIALITIES:*
*Arts & Crafts; Bodywork & Breathwork; Counselling; Health & Healing; Inner process; Meditation; Prayer.*

# Rumwood - Rest & Healing

Rumwood
Cardinal's Green
Horseheath
Cambridgeshire
CB1 6QX
Telephone: 01223 891729
Facsimile: 01223 892596

Amid the peaceful, rolling countryside of south Cambridgeshire, Mary and Robin welcome you into their warm and comfortable cedar-wood home - to relax, unwind and "just be" for a while. With spacious sunny rooms, expansive views, beautiful gardens, wonderful walks, a swimming pool and sauna - plus Reiki Healing, Traditional Thai Massage, Nature's Herbs for Health and Energy and Bach Flower Remedies - and - a loving atmosphere of caring and sharing, you can find space, rest, peace and positivity to re-charge your energies in "a little piece of paradise". "Beautiful people in a beautiful place." Chrissy. "Lovely to come to this peaceful cocoon. I'm going home rested and refreshed." Brenda. Weekend courses include the Findhorn Foundation "Game of Transformation", Reiki attunements and seminars and Peacemaking - between Women and Men, a powerful, exciting and enlightening One-Day Workshop co-facilitated by Robin and Mary. The vegetarian/vegan food is simply delicious and mealtime conversations are fascinating, fun and inspirational! "From Devas to Daffodils - the brightest conversation and the best coffee I've ever known!" Don. Rumwood is only one hour or so from London - by car or train - and less than two hours from Birmingham. To come and stay - and for more details - please give us a ring.

*ACCOMMODATION:*
*6 bedspaces in 3 rooms (includes 1 single); Group B&B; Group full board; Individual B&B; Individual full board; Large indoor*

*space; No smoking in building; Special diets.*
*EVENT TYPES:*
*Accredited courses; Guided group retreats; Guided individual retreats; Own course programme; Regeneration programmes; Self directed retreats.*
*SUITABILITY OR SPECIALISM:*
*Adults; Couples; Gay men; Lesbian women; Men; Older people; Women.*
*SUBJECT SPECIALITIES:*
*Health & Healing.*

---

# Wood Norton Hall

*Contact: Lorna & Hamish Barker*
*Wood Norton Hall*
*Hall Lane*
*Wood Norton*
*Norfolk*
*NR20 5BE*
*Telephone: 01362 683804*

Wood Norton Hall is a fine listed Georgian house with spacious comfortable rooms and sauna. Set in its own tranquil and private grounds of 3.5 acres. Eighteen miles from Norwich, ten miles from the north Norfolk coast. We have ten years experience in offering a varied programme of residential courses with delicious vegetarian food. Come and be part of the warm security of our family and home. Participate in an organised event or use us as a base for relaxation and visiting this beautiful area. Programme and brochure available.

SPIRITUAL ORIENTATION:
New Age.
ACCOMMODATION:
22 bedspaces in 8 rooms; Camping; Exclusively vegetarian; Group full board; Individual B&B; Individual self catering; Large indoor space; No smoking in building; Small spaces; Special diets; Venue for hire.
EVENT TYPES:
Accredited courses; Guided group retreats; Own course programme.
SUITABILITY OR SPECIALISM:
Adults.
SUBJECT SPECIALITIES:
Arts & Crafts; Bodywork & Breathwork; Counselling; Group Process; Health & Healing; Inner process; Meditation; Self expression.

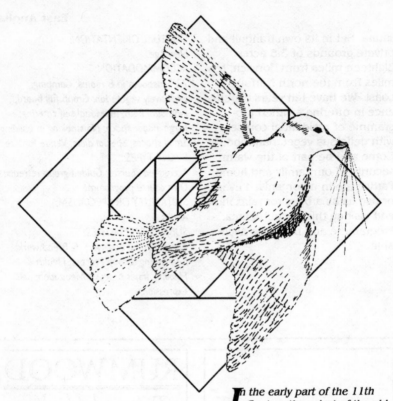

*I*n the early part of the 11th Century the priest of the old church of St Peter in Northampton had a very devout servant who he felt would benefit from a pilgrimage to Rome. The servant was already at the port when he had a dream in which he was ordered to return home. Once back he kept a vigil in the church and in another dream was told to search a particular part of the church where he found an ancient tomb. At midnight the church was filled with light and a snow-white dove appeared and sprinkled those watching with holy water. Alfgiva, a crippled girl, was miraculously cured and when the tomb was opened it was found to contain the bones of St Ragener.

# East Midlands

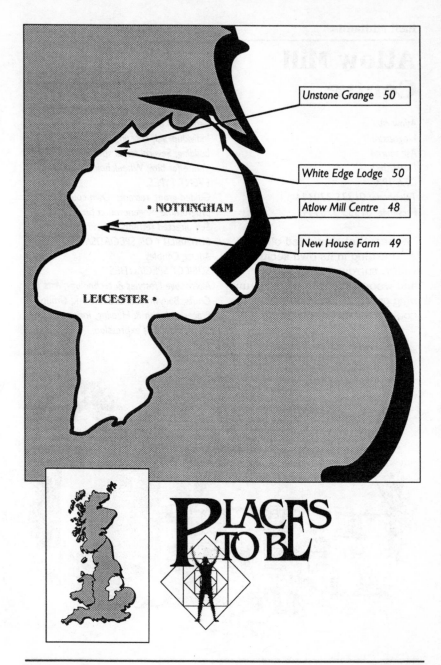

Unstone Grange 50

White Edge Lodge 50

• NOTTINGHAM

Atlow Mill Centre 48

New House Farm 49

LEICESTER •

# Places to Be

# Atlow Mill Centre

Atlow Mill
Hognaston
Ashbourne
Derbyshire
DE6 1PX
Telephone: 01335 370444
Facsimile: 01335 370444

A beautiful converted old mill nestling in its own secluded valley, surrounded by pasture and woodlands with a brook running gently by. Vegetarian home cooked meals or self-catering.

SPIRITUAL ORIENTATION:
New Age.
ACCOMMODATION:
23 bedspaces in 7 rooms (includes 4 singles); Camping; Exclusively vegetarian; Group full board; Group self-catering; Individual self catering; No smoking in building; Several small spaces; Special diets; Venue for hire; Wheelchair accessible.
EVENT TYPES:
Guided group retreats; Own course programme; Regeneration programmes; Self directed retreats; Working holidays.
SUITABILITY OR SPECIALISM:
Adults; Couples.
SUBJECT SPECIALITIES:
Alternative lifestyles & technology; Arts & Crafts; Bodywork & Breathwork; Group Process; Health & Healing; Inner process; Meditation; Self expression.

# New House Farm

Contact: Mary Smail
New House Farm
Kniveton
Ashbourne
Derbyshire
DE6 IJL
Telephone: 01335 342429

Organically managed, this traditional family farm is half a mile from a main road in a lovely location. Features include Bronze-age burials, quarry and wild-flower area. Free-range livestock and gardens provide for our own use and local sales. We are listed in The Permaculture Plot and are WWOOF hosts (working holidays). A converted hay-loft is a library and study. B&B ranges from £8 to £15.50 per night with extra pot-luck suppers, teas, babysitting and guided walks. There is space for caravans and tents. An old barn provides a venue for do-it-yourself courses. Permaculture, herbalism, archaeology etc especially suitable. Groups of 15 or more if bringing your own camp.

SPIRITUAL ORIENTATION:
Christian/Celtic.
ACCOMMODATION:
15 bedspaces in 6 rooms/caravans; Camping; Child friendly all ages; Child minding service; Group B&B; Individual B&B; Individual self catering; Large indoor space; No smoking in building; Several small spaces; Special diets; Venue for hire.
EVENT TYPES:
Self directed retreats; Working holidays.
SUITABILITY OR SPECIALISM:
Adults; Children under 12; Families with children; Young people 12 to 18.
SUBJECT SPECIALITIES:
Conservation work; Food & Horticulture.

# Unstone Grange

Unstone Grange
Crow Lane
Unstone
Derbyshire
S18 5AL
Telephone: 01246 412344

A centre for personal creative growth. Set in the lovely Derbyshire countryside, the atmosphere at Unstone Grange attracts those seeking a wider experience of life. We are used by community and youth groups of all types. They come to use our centre to access and express their creative spirit through dance, drama, craftwork, writing, painting, music, meditation, bodywork, healing and a wide range of other activities. From £12 per person per night self catering.

SPIRITUAL ORIENTATION:
New Age.
ACCOMMODATION:
32 bedspaces in 10 rooms; Camping; Group B&B; Group full board; Group self-catering; Large indoor space; Several small spaces; Special diets; Venue for hire.
EVENT TYPES:
Guided group retreats; Regeneration programmes; Working holidays
SUITABILITY OR SPECIALISM:
Adults; Couples; Families with children; Men; Women; Young people 12 to 18.
SUBJECT SPECIALITIES:
Alternative lifestyles & technology; Arts & Crafts; Bodywork & Breathwork; Counselling; Earth mysteries; Food & Horticulture; Group Process; Health & Healing; Inner process; Meditation; Prayer; Ritual & Shamanic; Self expression.

# White Edge Lodge

Contact: John Wragg
care of 8 Beaufort Road
Sheffield
S10 2ST
Telephone: 0114 267 0308

S ituated in a dramatic location in the Peak National Park, White Edge Lodge has breathtaking views of the Hope Valley and many peaks. This self-catering facility is basically a two-storey camping barn with fitted kitchen and furnished lounge with a wood stove. Ideal for personal or small groups retreats; a base for outdoor pursuits; parties; and as a young person's activity centre. Managed by the Flame Foundation - a registered charity (no 506106).

*ACCOMMODATION:*
*12 bedspaces in 3 rooms; Group self-catering; Individual self catering; Venue for hire.*
*EVENT TYPES:*
*Self directed retreats.*

*In 794 a man named Ethelbert fell in love with Alfrida, the daughter of Offa, King of Mercia. They were engaged to be married; but Offa's wife, Queen Cynethryth, was jealous of her daughter's happiness and persuaded Offa that Ethelbert should be murdered. So on the eve of the wedding, Ethelbert was ambushed and his head cut off. Wherever the head and body were buried miraculous lights appeared above the grave. When Ethelbert's remains were taken to Hereford for re-burial, a spring appeared at a spot where they had briefly touched the ground. This spring became known as St Ethelbert's Well.*

# West Midlands

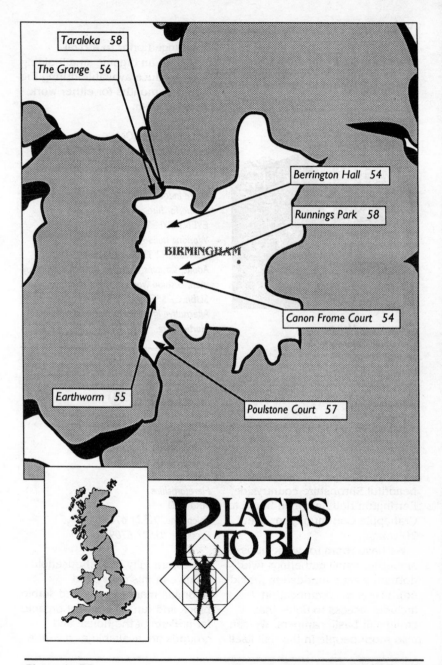

Taraloka 58

The Grange 56

Berrington Hall 54

Runnings Park 58

BIRMINGHAM

Canon Frome Court 54

Earthworm 55

Poulstone Court 57

# PLACES TO BE

# Berrington Hall 🌀

*Contact: any Member*
*Crabapple Community*
*Berrington Hall*
*Berrington*
*Shrewsbury*
*Shropshire*
*SY5 6HA*
*Telephone: 01743 761418*

Three miles outside Shrewsbury in 20 acres of beautiful Shropshire countryside, Berrington Hall has been home to Crabapple Community for over 20 years.

We have room for workshops and other small gatherings (with dormitary accommodation provided). Visitor accommodation includes access to fields that could suit basic campers. We can also room people in the Hall itself

if arranged prior to arrival.

We are an organic smallholding with produce available during the summer months for either work, trade or cash.

*ACCOMMODATION:*
*12 bedspaces in 3 rooms (includes 1 single); Camping; Child friendly all ages; Group self-catering; Individual self catering; Large indoor space; No smoking in building; Venue for hire.*
*EVENT TYPES:*
*Working holidays.*
*SUITABILITY OR SPECIALISM:*
*Adults; Couples; Families with children; Gay men; Lesbian women; Men; Women.*
*SUBJECT SPECIALITIES:*
*Alternative lifestyles & technology; Food & Horticulture.*

# Canon Frome Court 🌀

*Contact: The Secretary*
*Frome Society*
*Canon Frome*
*Ledbury*
*Herefordshire*
*HR8 2TD*
*Telephone: 01531 670717*
*Facsimile: 01531 670990*

A community of 18 households live in this converted Georgian manor house and stable block and run 40 acres of organic farm. Parts of the house and grounds are available as a venue for large and small events of all kinds. Facilities for hire include: kitchen, meeting room and large multi-purpose hall.

Prices vary depending on group size. Price guide for a group of 30 people: meeting room/kitchen, daily £25; weekly £150. Accommodation: Camping for around 100 by the lake (£3.00 /person), two double guest rooms (£8.50), bed only (£8.50) or B&B (£11.50) with members of the Community.

*ACCOMMODATION:*
*28 bedspaces in 14 rooms (includes 2 singles); Camping; Child friendly all ages; Group self-catering; Individual B&B; Large indoor space; Venue for hire.*
*SUITABILITY OR SPECIALISM:*
*Adults; Couples.*

# Earthworm

*Contact: Events Organiser*
*Earthworm Housing Co-op Ltd*
*Wheatstone*
*Dark Lane*
*Leintwardine*
*Shropshire*
*SY7 0LH*
*Telephone: 01547 540461*

Camping field (approximately 100 capacity) with covered catering/dining area. Three fire areas, running water, compost toilets, large cooker. A few indoor rooms/ workshops. Work commenced August 1994 to develop further indoor facilities. We improve the events facilities every year with any profit made from the previous season; aim to remain the best value for money "green" venue and accessible to those on low incomes. Act mainly as hosts but also run several small events ourselves. Seven acres with interesting house and outbuildings, Welsh Border of The Marches. Pretty, rural, close to village facilities. Accessible by public transport; 1.5 hours drive from Birmingham; 2 hours Bristol; 2.5 hours Manchester. Many attractive features: organic gardens, orchard, mature trees; many people find it a very spiritual place. Managed by a small co-operative community along ecological, organic, permacultural principles. Children welcome - suits outdoor fans. Ideal for practical crafts, horticulture, green gatherings and celebrations, permaculture, building and renovation. May allow special rates or free accommodation to course organisers in return for practical work/ skills/ tuition to residents. Rarely cook for large events - have contact/ arrangements with several catering co-ops. Prefer catering to be at least vegetarian. Site visit welcome by advance arrangement. Please contact us in writing with details/ requirements.

*SPIRITUAL ORIENTATION:*
*Celtic/Pagan.*
*ACCOMMODATION:*
*15 bedspaces in 3 rooms, Camping; Child friendly all ages; Exclusively vegetarian; Group full board; Group self-catering; Large indoor space; Several small spaces; Special diets; Venue for hire; Wheelchair accessible.*
*EVENT TYPES:*
*Accredited courses; Self directed retreats; Working holidays.*
*SUBJECT SPECIALITIES:*
*Alternative lifestyles & technology; Conservation work; Food & Horticulture.*

# The Grange

*Contact: Sheila Ward*
*The Grange, Ellesmere*
*Shropshire*
*SY12 9DE*
*Telephone: 01691 623495*

A Georgian house in ten acres of grounds on the Welsh borders near the Shropshire meres and canals. The Grange opened as a retreat house in 1987 with the primary aim of providing a space for women to explore the potential of the second half of life. However there is also a programme of events for men and women of all ages. There is a Natural Therapy Centre. The building (which was formerly a three star hotel) is sometimes available for groups with their own programme between March and October.

Poulstone Court, a spacious and comfortable Victorian country house, is a residential venue midway between Hereford and Ross-on-Wye. Five minutes' walk from the River Wye, it lies in lush, peaceful surroundings. The beautiful grounds include a walled garden and flat lawns perfect for outside activity. Sleeping accommodation is in attractively furnished one- to five-bedded rooms, with a self-contained flat ideal for facilitators. Two large workshop spaces in the house are complemented by a spacious barn, perfect for movement. All food is vegetarian. Poulstone Court is regularly used for courses in Tai Chi, meditation, psychotherapy, counselling, shamanism, movement and singing.

*SPIRITUAL ORIENTATION:*
*Christian/Inter-faith/New Awareness*
*ACCOMMODATION:*
*30 bedspaces in 17 rooms (includes 5 singles); Group B&B; Group full board; Individual B&B; Individual full board; Large indoor space; No smoking in building; Several small spaces; Special diets; Venue for hire; Wheelchair accessible.*
*EVENT TYPES:*
*Guided group retreats; Own course programme; Regeneration programmes; Working holidays.*
*SUITABILITY OR SPECIALISM:*
*Women.*
*SUBJECT SPECIALITIES:*
*Arts & Crafts; Bodywork & Breathwork; Counselling; Health & Healing; Inner process; Meditation; .*

# Poulstone Court

*Poulstone Court*
*Kings Caple*
*Herefordshire*
*HR1 4UA*
*Telephone: 01432 840251*
*Facsimile: 01432 840860*

*ACCOMMODATION:*
*33 bedspaces in 12 rooms (includes 1 single), Exclusively vegetarian; Group full board; Large indoor space; No smoking in building; Venue for hire.*
*EVENT TYPES:*
*Regeneration programmes.*
*PARTICIPANT TYPES:*
*Adults; Men; Women.*

# Runnings Park 🛥

Contact: Kay Wiseman
Runnings Park
Croft Bank
West Malvern
Worcestershire
WR14 4DU
Telephone: 01684 573868
Facsimile: 01684 892047

A Centre for Health, Healing and Self-Development. Nestled against the Malvern Hill this unique setting offers cosy, comfortable accommodation, peace and tranquility to singles and couples alike with a full programme of workshops and retreats throughout the year.

∗ Guests relax in the heated indoor pool, take a sauna or book a treatment at the Health and Relaxation Centre. Our restaurant tantalises your taste-buds with wholesome food to round off the Runnings Park experience.

∗ Trainers! Special workshop rates available upon request for group bookings.
ACCOMMODATION:
25 bedspaces in 22 rooms (includes 16 singles); Group B&B; Group full board; Individual B&B; Individual full board; Large indoor space; No smoking in building; Several small spaces; Special diets; Venue for hire.
EVENT TYPES:
Accredited courses; Guided group retreats; Own course programme; Self directed retreats; Teacher training.
SUITABILITY OR SPECIALISM:
Adults.
SUBJECT SPECIALITIES:
Health & Healing.

# Taraloka Buddhist Retreat Centre for Women ☸

Cornhill Farm
Bettisfield
Whitchurch
Shropshire
SY13 2LD
Telephone: 01948 710646
E-Mail: 100073.3502@compuserve.com

We run retreats, teaching meditation and Buddhism. Open to all women. Shared and

single rooms. Vegetarian/vegan food. Country walks, peace, friendship, fun!
*SPIRITUAL ORIENTATION:*
*Buddhist.*
*ACCOMMODATION:*
*30 bedspaces in 9 rooms (includes 3 singles); Exclusively vegetarian; Individual full board.*
*EVENT TYPES:*
*Guided retreats.*
*SUITABILITY OR SPECIALISM:*
*Women.*
*SUBJECT SPECIALITIES:*
*Meditation.*

*O*ne day Brochwel Ysgythrog, a prince of Powys, was hunting. His hounds were in pursuit of a hare but eventually the exhausted animal found shelter between the feet of a strange young woman standing in the forest. The hounds would not go near the woman. She told the prince that she was Melangell, and that she had come from Ireland to worship God. Realising that he was in the presence of a saint Brochwel gave Melangell land on which to build a chapel. St Melangell became the patron saint of hares and, in Montgomery, these creatures are sometimes known as *wyn bach Melangell*, or "Melangell's little lambs".

# Wales

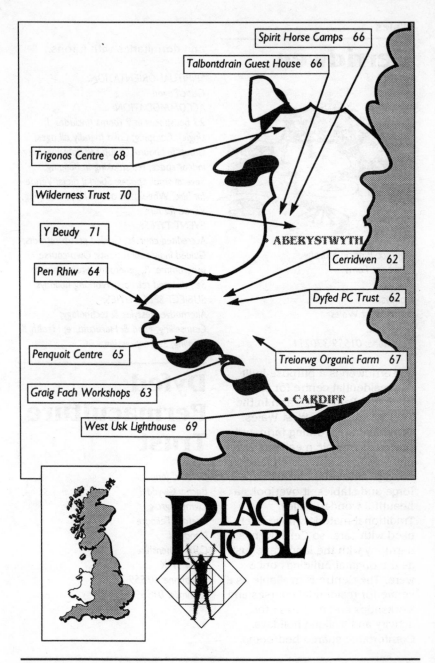

Spirit Horse Camps   66

Talbontdrain Guest House   66

Trigonos Centre   68

Wilderness Trust   70

Y Beudy   71

Pen Rhiw   64

Penquoit Centre   65

Graig Fach Workshops   63

West Usk Lighthouse   69

● ABERYSTWYTH

Cerridwen   62

Dyfed PC Trust   62

Treiorwg Organic Farm   67

● CARDIFF

# PLACES TO BE

# Cerridwen

Contact: Patricia Murphy
Penybanc Farm
Velindre
Llandysul
South West Wales
SA44 5XE
Telephone: 01559 370211

Cerridwen is a purpose-built residential centre for small groups at Penybanc Farm in the Teifi Valley, South West Wales. Penybanc is a working farm and produces organic meat and vegetables. The Centre itself is on the site of the old blacksmith's forge and stables, it overlooks a beautiful wooded valley. Traditional materials have been used with care, so Cerridwen is in harmony with the landscape just as the original buildings once were. The Centre is available as a venue for residential courses and workshops and as a base for activity and walking holidays. Comfortable shared bedrooms, and dormitaries with futons.

SPIRITUAL ORIENTATION:
Celtic/Pagan.
ACCOMMODATION:
23 bedspaces in 9 rooms (includes 1 single); Camping; Child friendly all ages; Group full board; Group self-catering; Large indoor space; No smoking in building; Several small spaces; Special diets; Venue for hire; Wheelchair accessible; ; Camping; Venue for hire.
EVENT TYPES:
Accredited courses; Guided group retreats; Guided individual retreats; Own course programme; Regeneration programmes; Self directed retreats; Working holidays.
SUBJECT SPECIALITIES:
Alternative lifestyles & technology; Counselling; Food & Horticulture; Health & Healing; Self expression.

# Dyfed Permaculture Trust

Contact: Jono
Bach y Gwyddel
Cwmpengraig
Drefach Felindre
Llandysul
Carmarthenshire
SA44 5HX
Telephone: 01559 371427
Facsimile: 01559 371427

**ACCOMMODATION:**
*Camping, Venue for hire.*
**EVENT TYPES:**
*Accredited courses, Guided group retreats, Guided individual retreats, Own course programme, Regeneration programmes, Self directed retreats, Working holidays.*
**SUBJECT SPECIALITIES:**
*Alternative lifestyles & technology, Counselling, Food & Horticulture, Health & Healing, Self expression.*

# Graig Fach Workshops

*Graig Fach*
*Llangennech*
*Llanelli*
*Dyfed*
*SA14 8PX*
*Telephone: 01554 759944*

A secluded 20 acre hillside farm with stone buildings, six fields (some rich in wildflowers and all bordered by wooded hedges), a stream, pond and woodland looking west across a valley to hill pastures and deciduous woods. Primarily a place where elements of sustainable living can be learnt and practiced, we offer basic facilities for running outdoor camps, courses or retreats but can provide catering, well-being support, childcare and guided retreats on request. We also run permaculture camps/courses. Camping fees are minimal but all who stay have the opportunity and are encouraged to join in farm projects for a couple of hours daily.

*Graig Fach continued*

Family small-holding and studio in woods above a river, an age and hill or two away from the South Wales coast and M4 motorway (Junction 48). Gateway to West and Mid-Wales. Walks from the door. Lakes, castles, sandy beach nearby. Art, crafts, writing, forestry, gardening, meditation in supportive setting. Instruction if required. Room for four indoors and camping space outside.

ACCOMMODATION:
*4 bedspaces in 2 rooms; Camping; Individual B&B; Individual full board.*
EVENT TYPES:
*Guided individual retreats.*
SUBJECT SPECIALITIES:
*Arts & Crafts; Food & Horticulture; Meditation.*

# Pen Rhiw

*Contact: Steve or Lis Cousens*
*Pen Rhiw*
*St David's*
*Pembrokeshire*
*Dyfed*
*SA62 6PG*
*Telephone: 01437 721821*
*Facsimile: 01437 721821*

Our purpose at Pen Rhiw is to provide a comfortable residential centre for groups, in a powerful and beautiful setting, with a friendly and welcoming atmosphere. The house itself is wonderful: there are twenty-two bedrooms giving up to thirty-four places; almost all have washbasins; there is central heating throughout and plenty of bathrooms and loos. The main group room is 50 x 16 ft, light and airy and with tremendous views of open countryside. There is a range of other spaces. We are situated just outside St David's in

the Pembrokeshire Coast National Park, an area of outstanding beauty with spectacular beaches and cliffs. Our vegetarian wholefood (much of the green veg grown in our organic garden) is delicious, plentiful and constantly praised. What people who come here (again and again) say is that they really appreciate the way that we make groups feel at home and safely relaxed and that we are around to meet people's needs without intruding into what the group is doing.

ACCOMMODATION:
*34 bedspaces in 22 rooms (includes 11 singles); Child friendly all ages; Exclusively vegetarian; Group full board; Large indoor space; Several small spaces; Special diets; Venue for hire; Wheelchair accessible.*
SUITABILITY OR SPECIALISM:
*All.*

# Penquoit Centre

*Contact: Joan Carlisle*
*Penquoit Centre*
*Lawrenny*
*Kilgetty*
*South Pembrokeshire*
*SA68 0PL*
*Telephone: 01646 651666*

The Centre can accommodate groups of ten to thirty in the converted longhouse. There is a fully equipped kitchen, dining room, two dormitories, campbeds, showers, toilets and long room for gatherings. Penquoit is on the boundary of the National Park and adjacent to Pencoed Farm which is fully organic. Self catering cost: £5 per person per night.

ACCOMMODATION:
*30 bedspaces in 2 rooms (includes 2 singles); Camping; Child friendly over 5; Group full board; Group self-catering; Individual self catering; Large indoor space; Venue for hire.*
EVENT TYPES:
*Self directed retreats; Working holidays.*
SUITABILITY OR SPECIALISM:
*All except the old and very young.*
SUBJECT SPECIALITIES:
*Arts & Crafts; Conservation work; Counselling; Earth mysteries; Food & Horticulture; Inner process; Meditation; Self expression.*

# Spirit Horse Camps

Contact: Erika Indra
19 Holmwood Gardens
London
N3 3NS
Telephone: 0181 346 3660

Spirit Horse Camps hosts spiritual retreats, performing arts and shamanic personal growth events camped out in wildest Wales (and Ireland) in traditional nomadic structures. Secluded amongst 3000 acres of ancient forest, rockpools, waterfalls, rock face, meadow and moor - a magical village of Turkoman yurts, tipis, huge Bedouin tents and chestnut domes (carpeted and with woodstoves) offers a superb undisturbed setting for teaching, dreaming, ceremony, meditation, male and female rites of passage, performing arts and rediscovering "the wild", within and without. Rates unbeatable. Write for a current programme.

*ACCOMMODATION:*
*85 bedspaces in 13 rooms; Camping; Child friendly over 5; Group full board; Group self-catering; Venue for hire.*
*EVENT TYPES:*
*Guided group retreats; Own course programme.*
*SUITABILITY OR SPECIALISM:*
*Adults; Men; Women.*
*SUBJECT SPECIALITIES:*
*Bodywork & Breathwork; Counselling; Earth mysteries; Group Process; Health & Healing; Inner process; Meditation; Outdoor activities & Sport; Prayer; Ritual & Shamanic; Self expression.*

# Talbontdrain Guest House

Contact: Hilary Matthews
Talbontdrain Guest House
Uwchygarreg
Machynlleth
Powys
SY20 8RR
Telephone: 01654 702192

Talbontdrain (thorn tree at the end of the bridge) is set in sheep pastures in the hills four miles outside Machynlleth. It is peaceful with plenty of space indoors and out. Excellent home cooked food, not exclusively vegetarian but mainly so and vegetarians are very welcome. There are children and animals here, all usually friendly! We are seven miles from the National Centre for Alternative Technology and it's easy to get here by train. Many excellent walks from the door. Comfortable sitting room with log fire and lots of books. Dining room with lovely round table. Fungus Feasts in the autumn and Women's Wilderness courses from time to time or on request if numbers are sufficient. Please ring for more details.

ACCOMMODATION:
6 bedspaces in 4 rooms (includes 2 singles); Camping; Child friendly all ages; Child minding service; Group B&B; Group full board; Individual B&B; Individual full board; No smoking in building; Several small spaces; Special diets.
EVENT TYPES:
Own course programme.
SPECIALISM:
Women.
SUBJECT SPECIALITIES:
Food & Horticulture; Outdoor activities & Sport.

# Treiorwg Organic Farm

*Contact: Jill Wolstenholme*
*Treiorwg*
*Trap*
*Llandeilo*
*Carmarthenshire*
*SA19 6RF*
*Telephone: 01558 823037*

Welcome to my piece of paradise! Treiorwg is a working organic farm set in the beautiful Brecon Beacons National Park. Your hostess is a winner of a national conservation award and a regular writer on organic farming. Meet the cattle, sheep, goats, pigs, hens, ducks, cats and donkey. Enjoy the abundant wildlife. Learn farming and conservation skills. Courses arranged to suit your needs. Comfortable "en famille" accomodation and good food: home-produced meat, eggs and milk and other organic produce. Weekend courses £80 per person including full board and tuition. Midweek or longer stays by arrangement.

*continued overleaf*

*Treiorwg Organic Farm continued*

ACCOMMODATION:
*4 bedspaces in 2 rooms; Camping;
Individual B&B; Individual full board; No
smoking in building.*
EVENT TYPES:
*Own course programme; Working holidays.*
SUITABILITY OR SPECIALISM:
*Adults; Couples.*
SUBJECT SPECIALITIES:
*Conservation work and farming; Outdoor
activities.*

# Trigonos Centre

*Plas Baladeulyn
Nantlle
near Caernarfon
Gwynedd
LL54 6BW
Telephone: 01286 882388
Facsimile: 01286 882424*

The Trigonos Centre is 7 miles from Caernarfon and 15 miles from Bangor. The site is of spectacular beauty - the buildings lying sheltered within 18 acres of fields and woodlands, overlooking a lake and through the foothills to Snowdon itself. Facilities include a large house, a purpose built arts centre, a seminar room (for up to 30), a hall suitable for events or exhibitions (for up to 50) and a library with a wide range of books available to visitors. Food is largely vegetarian/organic/biodynamic. Resident staff include people with experience in facilitating, action research, programme development, group work, community care, community development and horticulture. We run our own specialist courses but welcome all enquiries for use of the venue including from those who wish to develop new programmes collaboratively.

SPIRITUAL ORIENTATION:
Anthroposophical.
ACCOMMODATION:
28 bedspaces in 14 rooms (includes 4
singles); Camping; Child friendly all ages;
Group B&B; Group full board; Individual
B&B; Individual full board; Large indoor
space; No smoking in building; Several
small spaces; Special diets; Venue for hire;
Wheelchair accessible.
EVENT TYPES:
Own course programme; Self directed
retreats; Working holidays.
SUITABILITY OR SPECIALISM:
Adults; Families with children; Older people;
Young people 12 to 18.
SUBJECT SPECIALITIES:
Alternative lifestyles & technology; Arts &
Crafts; Conservation work; Food &
Horticulture; Group Process; Health &
Healing.

# West Usk Lighthouse

Contact: Frank & Danielle Sheahan
West Usk Lighthouse
St Brides
Wentloog
Newport
Gwent
NP1 9SF
Telephone: 01633 810126
Facsimile: 01633 815582

Situated between Newport and
Cardiff, the West Usk is a real
lighthouse, built in 1821 (now
Grade II listed) to a unique design
in order to house two families of
lighthouse keepers. The lighthouse overlooks the Bristol
Channel and the Severn Estuary
as well as the Welsh hills and valleys. All rooms are wedge-shaped,
with a slate bedded entrance hall
which leads to an internal collec-
tive well. The Lighthouse can
sleep ten and has workshop facilities in an outbuilding.

*continued overleaf*

*West Usk Lighthouse continued*

Couples, singles and children are most welcome. The atmosphere is peaceful and relaxing so it is an ideal place to unwind - either through the use of the flotation tank combined with an aromatherapy massage - or simply letting go. The Lighthouse is on crossing leys and has a certain *je ne sais quoi* about it. For the romantics there is a waterbed and four-poster bed (en suite rooms). Coastal walks (along deserted sea wall) and breathing fresh air is quite an inviting proposition to any city-dweller! Log fire in lounge in the winter, workshops on a regular basis: resident esoteric astrologer and tarot consultant and much more. Vegans and vegetarians catered for - non smoking establishment. From £20 B&B. Full tariff on request.

*SPIRITUAL ORIENTATION:*
*New Age.*
*ACCOMMODATION:*
*10 bedspaces in 6 rooms (includes 2 singles); Child friendly all ages; Group B&B; Individual B&B; No smoking in building; Venue for hire.*
*SUITABILITY OR SPECIALISM:*
*Adults; Couples; Families with children.*
*SUBJECT SPECIALITIES:*
*Health & Healing.*

# Wilderness Trust

*Contact: Frances Brockley*
*Waen Old Farmhouse*
*Llidiartywaen*
*Llanidloes*
*Powys*
*SY18 6JT*
*Telephone: 01686 413842*
*Facsimile: 01686 413842*

Informal, friendly, creative household running an organic smallholding. Sixteenth Century farmhouse set at 1000 ft in the rolling sheep farming country of mid-Wales. A retreat for any requiring a quiet creative place for spiritual growth (all disciplines welcome) and who wish to work in exchange for their keep. B&B £12 per night. Full board £18. Timber-framed barn suitable for self catering groups: £75 per week. Caravan (4 berth) from £50 per week.

*SPIRITUAL ORIENTATION:*
*Christian/Protestant.*
*ACCOMMODATION:*

12 bedspaces in 5 rooms; Camping; Child friendly all ages; Group self-catering; Individual B&B; Individual full board; Individual self catering; Large indoor space; No smoking in building; Several small spaces; Special diets; Venue for hire.
EVENT TYPES:
Self directed retreats; Working holidays.
SUBJECT SPECIALITIES:
Alternative lifestyles & technology; Conservation work.

# Y Beudy

Contact: Philippa Gibson
Y Beudy, Maes y Morfa
Llangrannog
Llandysul
Dyfed
SA44 6RU
Telephone: 01239 654561

Basic self-catering bunkhouse in converted farm building on organic smallholding, West Wales coast. Best for groups of about ten, can fit up to 20 if necessary. Beautiful area: cliff walks, beaches, village with shops, café 0.5 mile; dry-ski slope and other amenities nearby. Welsh-speaking area - Welsh learners especially welcome. Bring warm clothes and bedding. Accommodation: Large sleeping/day room upstairs (38 x 18 ft) with carpeting. Attractive space; timbered roof. Curtain to divide if wanted. Kitchen/dining downstairs; toilets/ washroom adjacent. Camp beds and mattresses. Some limited heating, and solar heated water. £3/person/night and electricity on meter. Booking essential.

ACCOMMODATION:
15 bedspaces in 2 rooms; Child friendly all ages; Group self-catering; Individual self catering; Large indoor space; Venue for hire.

# South West England

*T**he original church at Braunton
in Devon was founded by St
Brannoc, a 6th Century
missionary who was said to have
sailed from Wales in a stone coffin.
Apparently he was shown the site by
a sow and her piglets.
Many of his miracles involved
animals. On one occasion someone
stole his cow. They killed it and were
starting to cook it when Brannoc
called the cow. It immediately
emerged from the pot and
reassembled itself!*

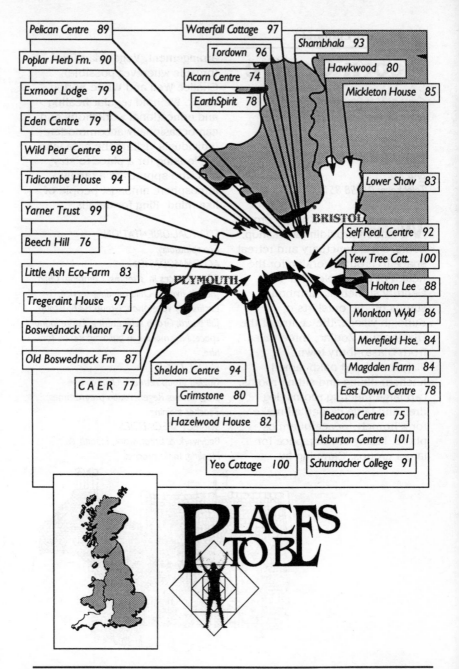

Pelican Centre 89

Waterfall Cottage 97

Shambhala 93

Poplar Herb Fm. 90

Tordown 96

Hawkwood 80

Acorn Centre 74

Mickleton House 85

Exmoor Lodge 79

EarthSpirit 78

Eden Centre 79

Wild Pear Centre 98

Tidicombe House 94

Lower Shaw 83

Yarner Trust 99

BRISTOL

Beech Hill 76

Self Real. Centre 92

Little Ash Eco-Farm 83

Yew Tree Cott. 100

PLYMOUTH

Holton Lee 88

Tregeraint House 97

Monkton Wyld 86

Boswednack Manor 76

Merefield Hse. 84

Old Boswednack Fm 87

Sheldon Centre 94

Magdalen Farm 84

CAER 77

Grimstone 80

East Down Centre 78

Hazelwood House 82

Beacon Centre 75

Asburton Centre 101

Yeo Cottage 100

Schumacher College 91

# Acorn Centre

*Contact: Mya Francesco*
*Acorn Centre*
*Butleigh*
*Glastonbury*
*Somerset*
*BA6 8SF*
*Telephone: 01458 851149*

We are a 'not for profit' organisation providing workshop, conference, sanctuary and retreat space to groups working for the health of the whole. Our 17th Century stonebuilt farmhouse stands on the outskirts of Butleigh village, the centre of the Glastonbury Zodiac, three miles from Glastonbury town. Flagstoned and oakbeamed kitchen; dining and sitting rooms; two large meeting rooms; log fires and large garden all make for a homely, peaceful atmosphere. Plenty of floorspace for larger groups. Camping by arrangement. Vegetarian food (organic wherever possible), Chalice Well and White Spring water. We hold regular healing and educational workshops and can occasionally accommodate individuals visiting the area who are looking for a place to stay and who appreciate a family atmosphere amongst people of like mind. Ring for details.

*SPIRITUAL ORIENTATION:*
*Eco-spirituality.*
*ACCOMMODATION:*
*10 bedspaces in 3 rooms; Camping; Child friendly over 5; Child minding service; Exclusively vegetarian; Group B&B; Group full board; Group self-catering; Large indoor space; No smoking in building; Venue for hire.*
*EVENT TYPES:*
*Guided group retreats; Own course programme; Regeneration programmes; Teacher training.*
*SUBJECT SPECIALITIES:*
*Bodywork & Breathwork; Health & Healing; Inner process.*

# The Beacon Centre ⚓

Contact: Wendy Webber
Cutteridge Farm
Whitestone
Exeter
Devon
EX4 2HE
Telephone: 01392 811203

The Beacon Centre, at Cutteridge Farm, is dedicated to Inner and Outer Peace. As a residential venue, we offer a warm and welcoming atmosphere for groups, and a variety of courses/ workshops/ retreats in personal growth and spiritual awak-

ening. Our setting (on 30 acres), amidst the lovely Devon Hills, yet only three miles from Exeter and a short distance from Dartmoor and the coast, is easily accessible by road/ rail. We have three lovely, good-sized group rooms, set around an attractive courtyard and a Sanctuary. Our accommodation is warm and comfortable with plenty of bathrooms. We offer catering (vegetarian and delicious) or self-catering facilities. Camping is possible. Other facilities include a Sauna, a trampoline, and a small "retreat" wood cabin by woodland and stream, ten minutes walk from the Centre. Therapies also available. Ask for a current brochure.

SPIRITUAL ORIENTATION:
New Age.
ACCOMMODATION:
30 bedspaces in 12 rooms; Camping; Child friendly all ages; Group B&B; Group full board; Group self-catering; Individual B&B; Individual self catering; Large indoor space; No smoking in building; Several small spaces; Special diets; Venue for hire.
EVENT TYPES:
Accredited courses; Guided group retreats; Guided individual retreats; Own course programme; Regeneration programmes; Self directed retreats; Working holidays;
SPECIALITIES:
Bodywork & Breathwork; Counselling; Group Process; Health & Healing; Inner process; Meditation; Self expression.

# Beech Hill Community

Contact: Dawn, Nik or Kathryn
Beech Hill
Morchard Bishop
near Crediton
Devon
EX17 6RF
Telephone: 01363 877587

Beech Hill is set in seven acres of grounds and gardens in a quiet, rural location midway between Dartmoor and Exmoor. Our newly converted course centre offers comfortable, small-dormitory accommodation; plus kitchen and lounge area with wood-burning stove. There are two large rooms with good workspace for dance, drumming, t'ai chi etc. A shady paddock provides good camping space. We offer superb wholefood catering using our own organic fruit and vegetables or, alternatively, courses can be self catered. An outdoor swimming pool is available in summer months.

ACCOMMODATION:
20 bedspaces in 5 rooms; Camping; Exclusively vegetarian; Group B&B; Group full board; Group self-catering; Individual B&B; Large indoor space; Special diets; Venue for hire; Wheelchair accessible.
EVENT TYPES:
Accredited courses; Self directed retreats.
SUITABILITY OR SPECIALISM:
Adults; Couples; Families with children; Gay men; Lesbian women; Men; Older people; Women; Young people 12 to 18.

# Boswednack Manor

Contact: Dr Elizabeth Gynn
Boswednack Manor
Zennor
St Ives
Cornwall
TR26 3DD
Telephone: 01736 794183

Peaceful guesthouse in wildest Cornwall overlooking the sea and moors. Organic garden. Meditation room. Guided wildlife walks, birdwatching and wild-flower weeks. Bed and Breakfast, vegetarian evening meals. No smoking throughout. Self catering cottage also available.

*SPIRITUAL ORIENTATION:*
*Buddhist/Vipassana.*
*ACCOMMODATION:*
*10 bedspaces in 5 rooms; Child friendly under 5; Group B&B; Individual B&B; Individual self catering; No smoking in building; Several small spaces; Special diets.*
*EVENT TYPES:*
*Self directed retreats.*
*SUITABILITY OR SPECIALISM:*
*Adults; Couples; Families with children.*

---

# CAER ⚓

Contact: Jo May
Rosemerryn
Lamorna
Penzance
Cornwall
TR19 6BN
Telephone: 01736 810530
E-mail: jomay@thenet.co.uk
World Wide Web:
http://www.thenet.co.uk/~jomay

CAER is near the sea, on the site of an Iron Age settlement, with 7 acres of woods, gardens, streams and a Gypsy caravan (see cover). In the grounds is a 2500 year old temple - the Fogou - recently investigated by Channel 4's Time Team. (A book 'Fogou, Gateway to the

Underworld' by Jo May, is published by Gothic Image.) This Cornish Area of Outstanding Natural Beauty has beautiful sandy beaches, spectacular coastal walks, quaint harbours, wild moors, lush valleys, and more ancient sites than anywhere else in Western Europe. Ask for CAER's Programme of residential workshops and retreats. Self-catering cottage also available.

*ACCOMMODATION:*
*24 bedspaces in 10 rooms (includes 4 singles); Child friendly all ages; Exclusively vegetarian; Group B&B; Group full board; Group self-catering; Individual B&B; Individual self catering; Large indoor space; No smoking in building; Special diets; Venue for hire; Wheelchair accessible.*
*EVENT TYPES:*
*Accredited courses; Guided group retreats; Own course programme; Regeneration programmes; Adults; Couples; Men; Women.*
*SUBJECT SPECIALITIES:*
*Bodywork & Breathwork; Counselling; Earth mysteries; Group Process; Inner process; Meditation; Ritual & Shamanic.*

---

# EarthSpirit

Contact: David Taylor
Lockyers Farm
Dundon
Somerton
Somerset
TA11 6PE
Telephone: 01458 272161
Facsimile: 01458 273796

Five miles from Glastonbury, EarthSpirit lies within the 'temenos' (sacred enclosure) of Avalon. Situated next to a wildlife reserve and a yew tree which is over 1,700 years old! EarthSpirit has a healing atmosphere but is not attached to any one tradition. We provide full facilities to groups of all kinds in our specially converted seventeenth century barn complex. The main hall is 52 feet long with oak timbers, reeds and stone walls. Mediaeval, but with modern comforts such as underfloor heating and a large wood stove. A high roof and skylights create a light, airy atmosphere. Neighbouring B&B and camping can boost numbers. Seven acres of fields and gardens. Sweat Lodge and hot tub available. Phone for photos. £22/24hrs food/bed. Hall hire £80/day.

EarthSpirit

SPIRITUAL ORIENTATION:
Eco-spirituality.
ACCOMMODATION:
21 bedspaces in 7 rooms (includes 2 singles); Camping; Exclusively vegetarian; Group B&B; Group full board; Large indoor space; No smoking in building; Several small spaces; Special diets; Venue for hire.
EVENT TYPES:
Accredited courses; Guided group retreats; Regeneration programmes; Teacher training.
SUITABILITY OR SPECIALISM:
Adults.

# East Down Centre

Contact: Richard Jones
East Down Centre, Dunsford
Exeter, Devon
EX6 7AL
Telephone: 01647 24041

Peaceful accommodation for small groups or workshops. No sharing with other groups. Self-catering or catered. Large group room. Sympathetically converted thatched barn set in beautiful country within the Dartmoor Nat. Park.

ACCOMMODATION:
17 bedspaces in 5 rooms (includes 1
single); Child friendly over 5; Group B&B;
Group full board; Group self-catering; Large
indoor space; Venue for hire.
EVENT TYPES:
Own course programme.

# The Eden Centre

Contact: Jenny Davis
Eden House
38 Lee Road
Lynton
Devon
EX35 6BS
Telephone: 01598 53440

The Eden Centre, set in an
unspoilt Area of Outstanding
Natural Beauty, offers retreats;
aromatherapy; reflexology; creative workshops; poetry; photog-
raphy. A small centre for healing
and creative development yet
part of a wider vision including
the work and impulse of Rudolph
Steiner. Brochure available. Also
individually priced self-catering.

SPIRITUAL ORIENTATION:
Anthroposophical.
ACCOMMODATION:
7 bedspaces in 3 rooms; Exclusively
vegetarian; Individual self catering; No
smoking in building.
SUITABILITY OR SPECIALISM:
Adults; Men; Older people; Women.

SUBJECT SPECIALITIES:
Arts & Crafts; Health & Healing;
Meditation; Prayer.

# Exmoor Lodge

Contact: Nigel Winter
Exmoor Lodge, Chapel Street
Exford, Somerset
TA24 7PY
Telephone: 01643 831694

Located in the heart of Exmoor
National Park, overlooking
Exford village green. Exclusively
vegetarian, vegan and non-smoking. Exmoor Lodge operates on
cruelty free principles combined
with healthy food. A set three
course evening meal is available
which is prepared fresh each day.
Exmoor Lodge is not licensed but
guest are welcome to bring their
own drinks. Three rooms are en-
suite and two share a bathroom.
B&B prices range from £16 to
£21 per person per night.
Reductions available November
to March, or for group bookings.

ACCOMMODATION:
9 bedspaces in 5 rooms (includes 1 single);
Exclusively vegetarian; Group B&B; Group
full board; Individual B&B; Individual full
board; No smoking in building; Special
diets; Venue for hire.
SUITABILITY OR SPECIALISM:
Adults; Couples.

# Grimstone Manor ✿

Grimstone Manor
Yelverton
Devon
PL20 7QY
Telephone: 01822 854358
Facsimile: 01822 854358

Grimstone Manor is a residential venue on the edge of Dartmoor. It is a very comfortable house with full central heating, an indoor swimming pool, jacuzzi and sauna. Set in over 20 acres of grounds, it offers each course exclusive use of all the facilities. Food is mainly vegetarian and drinks and snacks are available in the dining room 24 hours a day. The Manor is open to courses all year: it is used regularly for courses in yoga; shamanism; dance; psychotherapy and massage; and also offers a variety of holiday and working breaks.

ACCOMMODATION:
40 bedspaces in 13 rooms (includes 2 singles); Group full board; Large indoor space; Special diets; Venue for hire.
EVENT TYPES:
Group retreats; Own course programme; Working holidays.
SUITABILITY OR SPECIALISM:
Adults; Couples; Families with children; Men; Women.
SUBJECT SPECIALITIES:
Bodywork & Breathwork; Earth mysteries; Group Process; Health & Healing; Inner process; Meditation; Ritual & Shamanic; Self expression.

# Hawkwood College

Hawkswood College
Painswick Old Road
Stroud
Gloucestershire
GL6 7QW
Telephone: 01453 759034
Facsimile: 01453 764607

Hawkwood College, a Registered Charity, is an independent centre for adult education. It offers short courses to people of all ages and from all walks of life. An informal atmosphere is aimed at and no formal qualifications are needed to participate. Over and above courses which offer experience in music, science, arts and crafts, Hawkwood seeks to foster -

through a variety of courses and seminars - ways and means to a spiritual foundation of life to counterbalance the materialistic values which dominate most fields of human activity today. There is particular reference to the work of Rudolf Steiner. Hawkwood, an early 19th Century manor house built on an ancient site, is surrounded by its own extensive grounds. Situated at the head of a small Cotswold valley with a panoramic view down the Severn Vale it provides a beautiful and peaceful setting for an Adult Education Centre.

*SPIRITUAL ORIENTATION:*
*Anthroposophical.* `
*ACCOMMODATION:*
*52 bedspaces in 32 rooms (includes 15 singles); Group full board; Individual B&B; Individual full board; Large indoor space; No smoking in building; Several small spaces; Special diets; Venue for hire; Wheelchair accessible.*
*EVENT TYPES:*
*Guided group retreats; Own course programme; Regeneration programmes; Self directed retreats.*
*SUITABILITY OR SPECIALISM:*
*Adults; Couples; Men; Older people; Women.*
*SUBJECT SPECIALITIES:*
*Alternative lifestyles & technology; Arts & Crafts; Bodywork & Breathwork; Conservation work; Group Process; Health & Healing; Inner process; Meditation; Self expression.*

# Hazelwood House

*Loddiswell*
*near Kingsbridge*
*Devon*
*TQ7 4EB*
*Telephone: 01548 821232*
*Facsimile: 01548 821318*

The Hazelwood Estate is a place of extraordinary peace and beauty, in the heart of the South Devonshire countryside. There are 67 acres of woodland, meadows, riverbank and orchards which are ideal for walking, painting or simply relaxing. Hazelwood is perfect for rest and reflection and offers special care for the weary or convalescent.
Hazelwood House itself is early Victorian and is open 365 days a year offering accommodation and meals prepared from organic produce. Guests may enjoy the comfort of log fires during the winter or relax on the veranda in summer. Four holiday cottages spread over the Estate offer the possibility of self-catering accommodation. Concerts, cultural events and courses take place at Hazelwood throughout the year. We have a varied programme and would be pleased to put you on our mailing list.

*ACCOMMODATION:*
*51 bedspaces in 1 rooms; Individual B&B;*
*Individual full board; Individual self catering;*
*Special diets.*
*EVENT TYPES:*
*Own course programme.*
*SUBJECT SPECIALITIES:*
*Arts & Crafts; Self expression.*

# Little Ash Eco-Farm

*Throwleigh*
*Okehampton*
*Devon*
*EX20 2HY*
*Telephone: 01647 231394*
*E-Mail: mkileywo@ac.exeter.uk*

Experience ecological living. Wind power, own water, food. Courses: eco-agriculture, horses (working and riding), animal behaviour and welfare. Phone first. Numbers can be larger with camping.

*ACCOMMODATION:*
*5 bedspaces in 3 rooms; Camping;*
*Individual B&B; No smoking in building.*
*EVENT TYPES:*
*Self directed retreats.*
*SUBJECT SPECIALITIES:*
*Outdoor activities & Sport.*

# Lower Shaw Farm

*Contact: Kevin*
*Lower Shaw Farm*
*Old Shaw Lane*
*Shaw*
*Swindon*
*Wiltshire*
*SN5 9PJ*
*Telephone: 01793 771080*

Once a dairy farm, Lower Shaw is now a residential centre running its own programme of events and hiring out its facilities to groups and organisations. It has basic and homely accommodation, large group rooms and provides wholesome vegetarian food. It has large gardens and play spaces. It is readily accessible by rail or motorway and is close to the Avebury stones and the Ridgeway. Programme of courses and hire charge details available on request. We welcome telephone enquiries.

*ACCOMMODATION:*
*40 bedspaces in 15 rooms; Venue for hire.*
*EVENT TYPES:*
*Own course programme; Working holidays;*
*Food & Horticulture.*

# Magdalen Farm

Contact: Alison Adams
The Wessex Foundation
Magdalen Farm Centre
Winsham, Chard
Somerset
TA20 4PA
Telephone: 01460 30144
Facsimile: 01460 30177

Experience the new Magdalen Farm Centre. Welcome to a safe and inspiring environment for a wide variety of purposes, including conferences, seminars, training and other residentials.

Set on a 130 acre organic dairy and arable farm in the lush splendour of the Somerset and Dorset borders, the centre provides the ideal setting for creative training, reflective leaning or simply for unwinding and relaxing. The focus of our newly converted centre is an attractive courtyard of old stone and brick farm buildings. The finishes and fittings are to a high standard and the Centre can be adapted to a wide range of different purposes.

ACCOMMODATION:
35 bedspaces in 8 rooms; Group B&B; Group full board; Group self catering; Camping; Exclusively vegetarian; No smoking in building; Child friendly over 5; Wheelchair accessible; Large indoor space; Venue for hire.
EVENT TYPES:
Guided group retreats; Own course programme.
SUITABILITY:
All.
SUBJECT SPECIALITIES:
Arts & Crafts; Self expression; Outdoor activities; Conservation work; Alternative lifestyles & technology; Inner process; Group process; Meditation.

# Merefield House

East Street
Crewkerne
Somerset
TA18 7AB
Telephone: 01460 73112

Now established ten years, Merefield House has many of its original guests returning. The proprietor is a committed vegetarian and the emphasis is on plentiful imaginative cuisine. The house itself is a listed building of historic interest dating back, in parts, to the 16th Century. Rooms are spacious and comfortably furnished. The surrounding area is ideal for walking, touring,

National Trust garden visits or just relaxing in our large lounge or walled garden. Prices are based on half board from £25 per person with a 10% discount for weekly bookings. Three rooms, doubles and twins, one en suite.

*ACCOMMODATION:*
*6 bedspaces in 3 rooms; Exclusively vegetarian; Individual B&B; Special diets.*
*SUITABILITY OR SPECIALISM:*
*Adults.*

# Mickleton House 🐟💮

*Mickleton*
*Gloucestershire*
*GL55 6RY*
*Telephone: 01386 438251*
*Facsimile: 01386 438727*

A centre for courses, workshops or events which may assist individuals in their spiritual and creative lives. Situated in the Cotswold village of Mickleton, eight miles south of Stratford-upon-Avon, with good national access from all directions. Spacious, light and airy Garden Room suitable for many uses - a beautiful and magical container built to allow creative energy to work and move. Light, quiet and well-equipped Seminar Room also available. Mickleton House was established 16 years ago as the heart centre of 'The Emissaries', a spiritual association of people and a registered charity, whose purpose is to provide a place in consciousness where Spirit may be real and generative expression in everyday living. Full catering provided and accommodation available in conjunction with programmes offered. The Emissaries also stage their own workshops and courses. Brochures available.

*continued overleaf*

*Mickleton House continued*
ACCOMMODATION:
*15 bedspaces in 10 rooms (includes 5
singles); Child friendly all ages; Group B&B;
Group full board; Large indoor space; No
smoking in building; Several small spaces;
Special diets; Venue for hire.*
EVENT TYPES:
*Guided group retreats; Regeneration
programmes.*
SUBJECT SPECIALITIES:
*Earth mysteries; Group Process; Health &
Healing; Inner process; Meditation; Prayer.*

# Monkton Wyld Court ❀

*Charmouth
Bridport
Dorset
DT6 6DQ
Telephone: 01297 560342*

O ur Centre for Holistic
Education offers a wealth of
inspirational courses in the beauty and tranquility of our eleven
acre estate, three miles from the
sea.
ACCOMMODATION:
*34 bedspaces in 11 rooms; Exclusively
vegetarian; Group full board; Individual full
board; No smoking in building; Special
diets; Venue for hire.*
EVENT TYPES:
*Guided group retreats; Own course
programme; Self directed retreats; Teacher
training; Working holidays.*
SUBJECT SPECIALITIES:
*Arts & Crafts; Bodywork & Breathwork;
Group Process; Inner process; Ritual &
Shamanic; Self expression.*

---

# Old Boswednack Farm

*Contact: Pip MacFarlane*
*Old Boswednack Farm*
*Zennor*
*Cornwall*
*TR26 3DD*
*Telephone: 01736 798857*

Old Boswednack Farm is situated on the wild North Cornish coast, between St Ives and St Just, and near to the village of Zennor. The landscape is spectacular, with the sun setting over the Atlantic and the moon rising over the Bronze age field system and moors. Many of Cornwall's ancient sites are within walking distance through the fields and footpaths. The stone circles, fogous and beautiful holy wells make this a very special place to spend some time. We offer a large bright indoor workshop - studio space. A kitchen - dining room with wooden tables, cookers, fridge etc. Hot showers. Fresh herbs from the garden. Accomodation can be arranged in old

granite cottages and farmhouse, very comfortable and interestingly furnished. For the cottage accomodation, we would need plenty of notice. Bookings are from Saturday to Saturday. For the camping workshops, bookings can be of any duration. Please telephone if you wish for further information, or have any special requirements.

*SPIRITUAL ORIENTATION:*
*Celtic/Pagan.*
*ACCOMMODATION:*
*12 bedspaces (includes 2 single rooms), Camping; Group self-catering; Large indoor space; No smoking in building; Venue for hire.*
*EVENT TYPES:*
*Guided group retreats; Own course programme.*
*SUITABILITY:*
*Adults; Couples; Families with children; Gay men; Lesbian women; Men; Older people; Women; Young people 12 to 18.*
*SUBJECT SPECIALITIES:*
*Conservation work; Counselling; Earth mysteries; Drum & Dance; Ritual & Shamanic; Self expression.*

# Pastoral Centre at Holton Lee

*Holton Lee*
*East Holton*
*Poole*
*Dorset*
*BH16 6JN*
*Telephone: 01202 631063*
*Facsimile: 01202 631063*

Purpose built hides and shelters have been located in areas of specific interest for bird watching with specially constructed paths making them accessible to all. The beauty of Holton Lee is available to everyone who wishes for a special place to stay where they can relax and enjoy freedom to explore the countryside and spend time away from the busyness of everyday life and responsibilities.

Overlooking Poole Harbour, The Barn is a new building situated at Holton Lee, a very attractive 350 acre site, with a varied accessible landscape including: woodland, heath, foreshore, saltmarsh and reedbed. Many varied species of plants and animals live in the area, including several rare butterflies and birds.

• Short stay accommodation for up to eight guests in a specially designed and fully equipped building, suitable for people with disabilities, including electrically operated beds and bath, call system, hoists, minicom and loop system ...
• Varied programme of activities for those who wish to participate.

Creative Arts - including painting, pottery, spinning and creative writing. Environmental Education Personal growth - self development.

• Comfortable rooms including a sitting room with TV, video and stereo.

• Home-style cooking - special diets can be catered for.

• Evening events giving the opportunity to socialise and integrate ...

• Arranged outings to local places of interest ...

• Help with stress management ...

• Massage and aromatherapy.

• Counselling available on request.

• Carriage driving for the disabled - located within the grounds ...

• A personal care package can be arranged on request.

SPIRITUAL ORIENTATION:
*Christian.*

ACCOMMODATION:
*11 bedspaces in 7 rooms (includes 4 singles); Child friendly all ages; Group full board; Individual full board; No smoking in building; Several small spaces; Special diets; Venue for hire; Wheelchair accessible.*

EVENT TYPES:
*Guided group retreats; Guided individual retreats; Own course programme; Self directed retreats; Working holidays.*

SUITABILITY OR SPECIALISM:
*All.*

SUBJECT SPECIALITIES:
*Arts & Crafts; Bodywork & Breathwork; Conservation work; Counselling; Health & Healing; Inner process; Meditation; Outdoor activities & Sport; Prayer; Self expression.*

# Pelican Centre

*Details overleaf*

Pelican Centre
Ferlingmere House
St Mary's Road
Meare
Glastonbury
Somerset
BA6 9SP
Telephone: 01458 860536
Facsimile: 01458 860553

The Pelican Centre provides groups and individuals with a wide range of opportunities for personal and psychological development in welcoming surroundings. We offer our own courses, workshops and retreats, or the Centre is available for hire. Set on the Somerset Levels close to Glastonbury, Ferlingmere House is a delightful mediaeval building with a peaceful walled garden and orchard leading down to the River Brue. There are three group rooms, a bar, a dining room and a well-equipped art studio. The food is vegetarian with home-grown organic vegetables and homemade bread. Group of ten full board £40/person/night.

*ACCOMMODATION:*
*16 bedspaces in 10 rooms (includes 4 singles); Camping; Child friendly over 5; Exclusively vegetarian; Group B&B; Group full board; Group self-catering; Several small spaces; Special diets; Venue for hire.*
*EVENT TYPES:*
*Own course programme; Self directed retreats.*
*SUITABILITY OR SPECIALISM:*
*Adults; Lesbian women; Older people.*

*SUBJECT SPECIALITIES:*
*Arts & Crafts; Conservation work; Counselling; Inner process; Meditation; Self expression.*

# Poplar Herb Farm

*Contact: Richard or Christine Fish*
*Poplar Herb Farm*
*Burtle*
*Bridgwater*
*Somerset*
*TA7 8NB*
*Telephone: 01278 723170*

We offer exclusively vegetarian B&B accommodation in a peaceful and relaxing rural environment. Our two acre organic smallholding includes a herb nursery and unique astrological herb garden, and is also home to various rescued animals.

Tuition in meditation, astrology and herbalism can be arranged to suit the needs of individuals and small groups. Astrological counselling is available. Ideal environment for retreats. Our library and meditation room are available for the use of guests.

Only seven miles west of Glastonbury, Poplar Farm is situated on the Somerset Levels, an area renowned for its natural beauty and abundant wildlife.
*ACCOMMODATION:*

7 bedspaces in 3 rooms; Exclusively vegetarian; Group B&B; Individual B&B; No smoking in building; Special diets.
EVENT TYPES:
Guided group retreats; Guided individual retreats.
SUITABILITY OR SPECIALISM:
Adults; Couples.
SUBJECT SPECIALITIES:
Counselling; Food & Horticulture; Inner process; Meditation.

# Schumacher College

Contact: Hilary Nicholson
Schumacher College
The Old Postern
Dartington
Totnes
Devon
TQ9 6EA
Telephone: 01803 865934
Facsimile: 01803 866899

Situated on the beautiful Dartington Hall Estate, this international centre for ecological studies runs one- to five-week residential courses on: ecological economics and development issues; the links between philosophy, psychology and ecology; and the new understandings emerging from recent scientific discoveries. Courses are led by world-renowned writers and teachers, including Fritjof Capra, James Hillman, Vandana Shiva and Helena Norberg-Hodge. Course participants aged from 20 to over 80 come to the College from all over the world and, to balance the intellectual inquiry, share in the everyday tasks of running the College. A craft room and excellent library.

SPIRITUAL ORIENTATION:
Eco-spirituality.
ACCOMMODATION:
25 bedspaces in 10 rooms; Exclusively vegetarian; No smoking in building; Wheelchair accessible.
EVENT TYPES:
Own course programme; Accredited courses.
SUITABILITY OR SPECIALISM:
Adults.

# Self Realization Meditation Healing Centre

*Laurel Lane*
*Queen Camel*
*Somerset*
*BA22 7NU*
*Telephone: 01935 850266*
*Facsimile: 01935 850234*

The Centre is a charitable trust founded by Mata Yoganandaji to help people - of all beliefs and none - find peace and fulfillment. Run by a spiritual family of teachers, healers and counsellors, providing courses, individual appointments, retreats and nurturing breaks, it is a spiritual home in every sense - with unconditional love as the watchword. Meditation courses are held regularly and all are welcome to join the morning and evening meditations. There are three acres of beautiful gardens, log fires in winter, a library and therapy pool. Home-cooked vegetarian meals - special diets catered for. Please ask for a brochure and full course programme, including Professional Healer and Counsellor Training, Self

Development, Hatha and Aqua Yoga. Weekend courses: £96; Week courses: £289.75; Easter/Christmas Retreats: £78; all with Full Board. B&B from £15.50 per night; Full Board from £28.50 daily.

ACCOMMODATION:
*14 bedspaces in 10 rooms (includes 6 singles); Child friendly all ages; Exclusively vegetarian; Individual B&B; Individual full board; Individual self catering; Large indoor space; No smoking in building; Several small spaces; Special diets.*
EVENT TYPES:
*Accredited courses; Guided group retreats; Guided individual retreats; Own course programme; Regeneration programmes; Self directed retreats; Teacher training.*
SUITABILITY AND SPECIALISMS:
*Adults; Children under 12; Couples; Families with children; Older people; Young people 12 to 18.*
SUBJECT SPECIALITIES:
*Bodywork & Breathwork; Counselling; Health & Healing; Inner process; Meditation; Prayer; Self expression.*

# Shambhala Healing Centre

*Contact: Anna Khan*
*Shambhala Healing Centre*
*Coursing Batch*
*Glastonbury*
*Somerset*
*BA6 8BH*
*Telephone: 01458 833081*
*Facsimile: 01458 834751*
*E-Mail: shambhala@dial.pipex.com*
*World Wide Web:*
*http://www.isleofavalon.co.uk/shambala.html*

We welcome you to our Healing Centre to enjoy our wood-burning sauna, large seven-seater jacuzzi set in a conservatory full of exotic plants, Aromatherapy massage, Shiatsu massage, Reiki Healing, Rebirthing and in-depth counselling. We are a team of dedicated, sensitive, loving healers and would especially recommend one of our *Intensive Healing Breaks*, when you'll be pampered and cared for completely. Staying in the Shambhala Guest House is an intense and loving experience and you have the choice of an Egyptian, Tibetan or Chinese bedroom. We also cook wonderful vegetarian lunches and suppers. Shambhala is a sacred site and we have a beautiful twelve-point-ed Crystal Star which marks the Heart of the Heart. People come from all over the world to visit our centre and we know you will enjoy it and receive great benefit from your visit. Sited on the wooded slopes of the Tor, we look over the magnificent Vale of Avalon and you can enjoy our gardens, with pond and waterfall, and our flock of white doves. Inspiring, welcoming, restful and fun! Weekly spiritual retreats. weekend courses in healing, channelling and higher consciousness. We also organise sacred journeys to Egypt, Israel and India.

*SPIRITUAL ORIENTATION:*
*New Age*
*ACCOMMODATION:*
*8 bedspaces in 4 rooms; Child friendly all ages; Exclusively vegetarian; Group B&B; Group full board; Individual B&B; Individual full board; Large indoor space; No smoking in building; Special diets.*
*EVENT TYPES:*
*Accredited courses; Guided group retreats; Guided individual retreats; Own course programme; Regeneration programmes; Self directed retreats; Teacher training; Working holidays.*
*SUBJECT SPECIALITIES:*
*Bodywork & Breathwork; Counselling; Group Process; Health & Healing; Inner process; Meditation; Prayer; Self expression.*

# The Sheldon Centre

Contact: Hillary Hanson
The Sheldon Centre
Dunsford
Exeter
Devon
EX6 7LE
Telephone: 01647 252203

Sheldon offers self-catering accommodation for groups in attractive converted farm buildings suitable for family, young people and adult groups. An ideal place to run your own event in the peace and quiet of the Devon countryside, with fields, woodland, hills and valleys all around. Sheldon is staffed by a small resident Community of lay Christians. We welcome guests of any faith or none. Our own pro-

gramme of quiet days, workshops and retreats is held each Spring and Autumn - please ask for details.

*SPIRITUAL ORIENTATION:*
*Christian.*
*ACCOMMODATION:*
*50 bedspaces in 18 rooms (includes 8 singles); Camping; Child friendly all ages; Group self-catering; Individual self catering; Large indoor space; No smoking in building; Special diets; Venue for hire.*
*EVENT TYPES:*
*Own course programme; Self directed retreats; Working holidays.*
*SUITABILITY OR SPECIALISM:*
*Adults; Children under 12; Families with children; Older people; Young people 12 to 18.*
*SUBJECT SPECIALITIES:*
*Counselling; Inner process; Meditation; Prayer.*

# Tidicombe House

Contact: Cheryl or Edward Thornburgh
Tidicombe House
Arlington
near Barnstaple
Devon
EX31 4SP
Telephone: 01271 850626
Facsimile: 01271 850626

Tidicombe lies peacefully secluded amidst hills and woods. There are walks, Riding

Stables and the beautiful grounds of Arlington Court (National Trust) nearby. Exmoor and the sea lie within a few miles, the coastline varying from wooded gorges descending between precipitous cliffs, to surfing beaches where Atlantic breakers roll onto miles of flat sands. There are tucked-away villages to explore and of course clotted cream and scones to indulge in! We offer vegetarian B&B - and sometimes full board. (Sorry, no pets or smoking). Our household is informal and we enjoy sharing meals with our guests. There is plenty of quiet space if you need it and if you want to join in gardening or feeding the chickens you will be welcome! We are renovating our outbuildings to house workshop space, art/craft studios etc. There is meditation space in the Barn and a Solar Dome In the Orchard. We have nearly five acres of fields and gardens. We are involved in organic gardening/permaculture, desktop publishing, painting. crafts, folk music, Devon Local Agenda 21 and North Devon L.E.T.S. Please write, phone or fax for more information.

*ACCOMMODATION:*
*Exclusively vegetarian; Individual B&B; No smoking in building; Venue for hire.*
*EVENT TYPES:*
*Self directed retreats.*

# Tordown B&B and Healing Centre

Situated on the southern slopes of the Tor overlooking the Vale of Avalon. Television, basin, tea and coffee making facilities in all rooms, with many en suite. Vegetarian, no smoking, own car park, garden, patio with glorious views, waterfall and pond. Two Reiki Masters in residence (Usul and Karuna). Also available for Ear Candeling and Higher Self Communication Sessions. Family run with a welcoming, friendly, peaceful and spiritual atmosphere. Varied accommodation. Choose from our Aquamarine, Jade and Amethyst Rooms or our Rose Quartz, Onyx, Lapis and Opal Suites. Library containing some of the oldest and newest spiritual/ healing books. A place to be peaceful, refind yourself, relax and enjoy.

SPIRITUAL ORIENTATION:
New Age.
ACCOMMODATION:
15 bedspaces in 7 rooms (includes 2 singles); Child friendly all ages; Exclusively vegetarian; Group B&B; Individual B&B; Large indoor space; No smoking in building; Venue for hire.
EVENT TYPES:
Accredited courses; Own course programme; Teacher training.
SUITABILITY OR SPECIALISM:
Adults; Children under 12; Couples; Families with children; Men; Older people; Women; Young people 12 to 18.
SUBJECT SPECIALITIES:
Counselling; Health & Healing; Meditation.

Contact: Cheryl or Michael Penn
Tordown
5 Ashwell Lane
Glastonbury
Somerset
BA6 8BG
Telephone: 01458 832287
Facsimile: 01458 831100

# Tregeraint House

*Contact:* Sue & John Wilson
*Tregeraint House*
*Zennor*
*St Ives*
*Cornwall*
*TR26 3DB*
*Telephone: 01736 797061*
*Facsimile: 01736 797061*

A roomy traditional granite cottage in a magnificent situation overlooking sea and hills. Warm, friendly place. All diets catered for.

*ACCOMMODATION:*
*8 bedspaces in 4 rooms (includes 1 single);*
*Child friendly all ages; Group B&B;*
*Individual B&B; No smoking in building;*
*Special diets; Venue for hire.*
*SUITABILITY OR SPECIALISM:*
*All.*

# Waterfall Cottage Healing Centre

*20 Old Wells Road*
*Glastonbury*
*Somerset*
*BA6 8ED*
*Telephone: 01458 831707*

Bed and Breakfast in a beautiful 17th Century cottage radiating peace and harmony; affirming country walks. Ten minutes walk: Tor, Chalice Well, Abbey, town centre. Library of spiritual/healing books. Use of garden and patio. All diets. Therapies/workshops in inner growth; crystal healing; flower essences; regression. Gentle, nurturing, unwind, recharge. Centre for exploring Avalon, ancient sites cloaked in myth, legend associated with Joseph of Aramathea, Holy Grail, King Arthur, Michael Line, Glastonbury Zodiac. Sweet Track (4000 BC) and nature reserve nearby. Maps, guides available. Tours arranged including Avebury, Camelot, Stonehenge, Tintagel. Coast 15 miles; One hour drive to South Dorset/Devon coast.

*continued overleaf*

*Waterfall Cottage continued*

*SPIRITUAL ORIENTATION:*
*New Age.*
*ACCOMMODATION:*
*6 bedspaces in 4 rooms (includes 1 single);*
*Exclusively vegetarian; Individual B&B; No*
*smoking in building; Special diets.*
*EVENT TYPES:*
*Guided group retreats; Guided individual*
*retreats; Regeneration programmes.*
*SUBJECT SPECIALITIES:*
*Bodywork & Breathwork; Earth mysteries;*
*Group Process; Health & Healing; Inner*
*process; Meditation.*

# Wild Pear Centre

*King Street*
*Combe Martin*
*Devon*
*EX34 0AG*
*Telephone: 01271 883086*

A centre for personal growth work located in a seaside village on the edge of Exmoor National Park and close to spectacular coastal scenery and secluded beaches. With a large group room and communal hall, generously equipped with cushions, work mattresses and a piano, the centre is a suitable workshop venue for a variety of group activities such as yoga, meditation, growth groups, bodywork, movement and dance.

Available for hire for residential or non-residential use (full board or self-catered) at reasonable rates, the centre also welcomes individual or group retreats or groups on holiday.

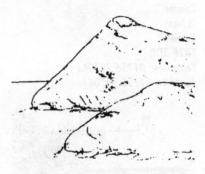

*ACCOMMODATION:*
*25 bedspaces in 8 rooms (includes 5*
*singles); Group B&B; Group full board;*
*Group self-catering; Individual B&B;*
*Individual self catering; Large indoor space;*
*Several small spaces; Special diets; Venue*
*for hire.*
*EVENT TYPES:*
*Self directed retreats.*
*SUITABILITY OR SPECIALISM:*
*Adults.*
*SUBJECT SPECIALITIES:*
*Bodywork & Breathwork; Counselling;*
*Group Process; Inner process; Meditation;*
*Self expression.*

# The Yarner Trust

*Contact: Franceska Hannis*
*The Yarner Trust*
*Welcombe Barton, Welcombe*
*Bideford, Devon*
*EX39 6HG*
*Telephone: 01288 331692*

We are based at Welcombe Barton, a stunning mediaeval farmhouse dating back to the Domesday Book. Only a mile from the North Devon coast, in an area of outstanding natural beauty, we are renovating the Barton into a residential centre. The Yarner Trust seeks to educate and empower people in the skills of sustainable living. The practical application and demonstration of pioneering ideas, coupled with an educational programme for the local community, colleges and residential visitors, forms the basis of the Trust's work. We are running courses on rural crafts, smallholding skills and

Permaculture, Deep Ecology etc. Our three acres of land are managed organically and we are currently developing a wildlife walk, forest garden and tree nursery. At present, accommodation will vary depending on the renovation process. We have five bedspaces in the main building and another six in the outbuildings, when they are completed. There is also the option of camping in spring and summer. Prices will vary, please write/ phone for information and an up-to-date newsletter.

*ACCOMMODATION:*
*5 bedspaces in 3 rooms; Camping;*
*Exclusively vegetarian; Group full board;*
*Group self-catering; Large indoor space; No*
*smoking in building; Several small spaces;*
*Venue for hire.*
*EVENT TYPES:*
*Accredited courses; Own course*
*programme; Self directed retreats.*
*SUITABILITY OR SPECIALISM:*
*Adults.*
*SUBJECT SPECIALITIES:*
*Alternative lifestyles & technology; Arts &*
*Crafts; Conservation work; Food &*
*Horticulture.*

# Yeo Cottage

Contact: Michael Cox
Yeo Cottage, Sandwell Lane
Totnes, Devon
TQ9 7LJ
Telephone: 01803 868157

Ideal for relaxation and stress relief or a general holiday. The cottage is in a lovely part of Devon only two miles from Totnes. Healing, meditation, relaxation and counselling is available free and there are many other therapies available in Totnes. This is a place to unwind and recharge yourself, and put your feet up. Lovely walks in a peaceful environment as well as sailing in Torbay. Bed and Breakfast rates are £14 per person per night. Evening meals available.

SPIRITUAL ORIENTATION:
New Age.
ACCOMMODATION:
6 bedspaces in 3 rooms; Individual B&B;
Individual full board.

EVENT TYPES:
Own courses; Self directed retreats.
SUITABILITY OR SPECIALISM:
Adults.
SUBJECT SPECIALITIES:
Health & Healing; Outdoor activities.

# Yew Tree Cottage

Contact: John Churchill
Yew Tree Cottage
Grove Lane, Redlynch
Salisbury, Wiltshire
SP5 2NR
Telephone: 01725 511730

A spacious cottage in a large garden overlooking a grazing paddock, in the pretty "New Forest" heritage village of Redlynch, near Salisbury. Excellent southern exploration base. Superb for quiet walking on farm and downland footpaths, or in the New Forest with its heaths, trees and abundant wildlife. Individual B&B with 3 rooms, 1 double, 1 twin, 1 single.

Traditional, vegetarian, vegan and others. (Evening meals can be booked in Redlynch). £17 nightly inc VAT. Child friendly over and under 5. Ample parking. Regret no smoking. Private hands-on healing and massage available (Japanese, Indian, traditional). Also health library.

*ACCOMMODATION:*
*5 bedspaces in 3 rooms (includes 1 single); Child friendly all ages; Individual B&B; No smoking in building; Special diets.*
*SUBJECT SPECIALITIES:*
*Health & Healing.*

# Ashburton Centre 🚣

**... LATE ENTRY ...**
*Contact: Stella West-Harling*
*Ashburton Centre for Holistic Education and Training*
*79 East Street*
*Ashburton, Devon*
*TQ13 7AL*
*Telephone: 01364 652784*
*Facsimile: 01364 653825*

A restored Georgian townhouse and nearby cottage, the Centre is a non-denominational spiritual community offering a wide variety of short courses and professional trainings from Vegetarian Cookery Weekends to Shiatsu, Voice Workshops, Healing Arts and New Year Celebrations. Twin *en suite* rooms, pool oppo-

site, close to Dartmoor and Totnes. Most of the food is organic from our own allotments. Shiatsu and nutritional healing therapies available. Bursaries available. We welcome all.

*ACCOMMODATION:*
*20 beds in 8 rooms; Individ B&B; Individ full board; Group full board; Group self catering; Exc vegtn; No smoking; Special diets; Large indoor space; Small spaces; Venue for hire.*
*EVENT TYPES:*
*Accredited courses; Guided group retreats; Own courses; Regeneration programmes.*
*SUITABILITY:*
*Adults.*
*SUBJECT SPECIALITIES:*
*Bodywork & Breathwork; Health & Healing; Food; Counselling; Inner process; Group process; Meditation.*

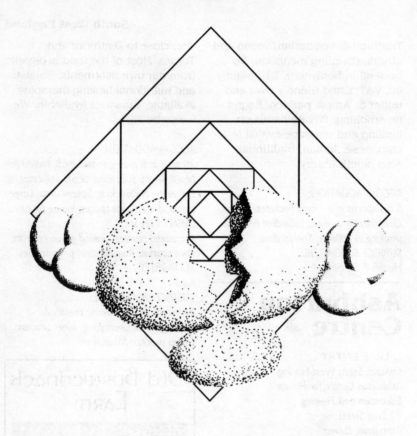

*D*uring the period that St Swithun was Bishop of Winchester (in the 9th Century) he is said to have performed many miracles. One day, apparently, an old woman dropped her basket of eggs on the ground. Swithun was passing by at the time and was so moved by the poor woman's plight that he made the eggs reform. The altar screen in the cathedral shows the saint with a pile of eggs at his feet. Each of the four candlesticks in his shrine has a broken eggshell at its base.

# South East England

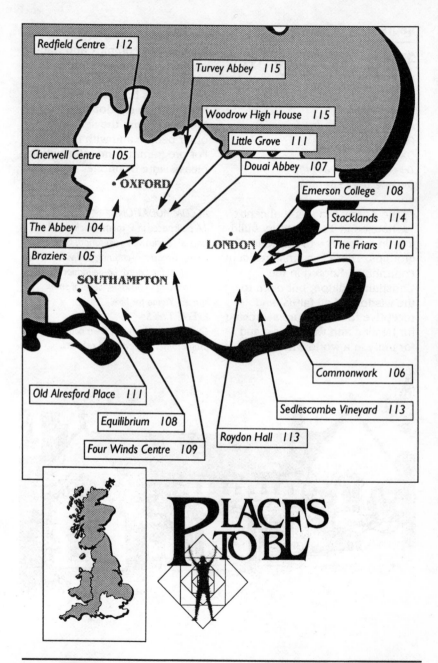

Redfield Centre   112

Turvey Abbey   115

Woodrow High House   115

Little Grove   111

Cherwell Centre   105

Douai Abbey   107

OXFORD

Emerson College   108

Stacklands   114

The Abbey   104

The Friars   110

Braziers   105

LONDON

SOUTHAMPTON

Old Alresford Place   111

Commonwork   106

Equilibrium   108

Sedlescombe Vineyard   113

Four Winds Centre   109

Roydon Hall   113

PLACES TO BE

# The Abbey 🌀

*The Abbey*
*Sutton Courtenay*
*Abingdon*
*Oxfordshire*
*OX14 4HF*
*Telephone: 01235 847401*
*Facsimile: 01235 847608*

The Abbey is a spiritual centre housed in 13th Century buildings in four acres of peaceful grounds. There is a small resident community. Rooted in the Christian tradition, but open to the wisdom of all faiths, and receptive to all who are searching for healing and wholeness, and for unity in a world which is increasingly complex and fragmented. The Abbey's programme is guided by a vision which emphasises the development of the four true relationships: with the divine, with the self, with other people and with the earth. For programme and information please write or phone.

*ACCOMMODATION:*
*14 bedspaces in 9 rooms (includes 4 singles), Exclusively vegetarian; Group full board; Group self-catering; Individual B&B; Individual full board; Large indoor space; No smoking in building; Several small spaces; Venue for hire.*
*EVENT TYPES:*
*Guided group retreats; Own course programme; Self directed retreats.*

# Braziers Adult College

Braziers Park
Ipsden, Wallingford
Oxfordshire
OX10 6AN
Telephone: 01491 680221

Residential college in 17th Century listed building - run by a small resident community with voluntary help from tutors and overseas students. Courses offered in Arts and Crafts; Social Sciences and Philosophy. Informal atmosphere. Visitors of all ages and persuasions welcome.

*ACCOMMODATION:*
*19 bedspaces in 13 rooms (includes 8 singles); Camping; Group B&B; Group full board; Ind. B&B; Ind. full board; Several small spaces; Special diets; Venue for hire.*
*EVENT TYPES:*
*Own course programme; Adults.*
*SUBJECT SPECIALITIES:*
*Arts & Crafts; Bodywork & Breathwork; Conservation work; Group Process; Health & Healing; Inner process; Self expression.*

# Cherwell Centre

*14-16 Norham Gardens*
*Oxford*
*OX2 6QB*
*Telephone: 01865 52106*
*Facsimile: 01865 58183*

The Cherwell Centre is run by members of the Society of the Holy Child Jesus, an international community of Catholic women. We work to provide a place of Christ-centred hospitality and an atmosphere of freedom and peace. The Centre, in North Oxford, is pleasantly situated, adjacent to the University Parks. Oxford City Centre is only ten minutes walk away.

*SPIRITUAL ORIENTATION:*
*Christian/Catholic.*

*Cherwell Centre continued*

ACCOMMODATION:
*29 bedspaces in 21 rooms (includes 13 singles); Group B&B; Group full board; Individual B&B; Individual full board; Large indoor space; No smoking in building; Several small spaces; Special diets; Venue for hire.*
EVENT TYPES:
*Guided group retreats; Guided individual retreats; Own course programme; Regeneration programmes; Self directed retreats.*
SUITABILITY OR SPECIALISM:
*Adults; Couples; Women.*
SUBJECT SPECIALITIES:
*Counselling; Inner process; Meditation; Prayer.*

# Commonwork

Bore Place
Chiddingstone
Kent
TN8 7AR
Telephone: 01732 463255
Facsimile: 01732 740264

Commonwork, an educational trust, is a place for conferences, workshops and seminars set on a 500 acre working farm in the Kentish Low Weald, near Sevenoaks. An old manor house with its ancient walled garden, and a group of historic barns within a courtyard, have been renovated and converted to provide a beautiful and peaceful environment. We can accommodate up to 50 residents, or 4 to 100 people for daytime visits. Tutors are available to groups for pottery, painting, shiatsu and guided walks. Our spaces are also suitable for dance and drama. Please talk to us about your specific requirements.

ACCOMMODATION:
*50 bedspaces in 27 rooms (includes 7 singles); Camping; Child friendly all ages; Group B&B; Group full board; Group self-catering; Individual B&B; Individual self catering; Large indoor space; No smoking in building; Several small spaces; Special diets; Venue for hire; Wheelchair accessible.*
EVENT TYPES:
*Own course programme.*
SUITABILITY OR SPECIALISM:
*Adults; Children under 12; Young people 12 to 18.*
SUBJECT SPECIALITIES:
*Arts & Crafts; Bodywork & Breathwork; Conservation work.*

# Douai Abbey

*Upper Woolhampton*
*Reading*
*Berkshire*
*RG7 5TQ*
*Telephone: 0118 971 5300*
*Facsimile: 0118 971 5203*

B enedictine Monastery offering hospitality and day conference facilities to individuals, small groups and workshops. Situated on the North Wessex Downs in an area of outstanding natural beauty. Good network of footpaths for walking. A variety of accommodation is available including single rooms, hostel and dormitory. Meals can be provided or self-catering facilities available. Further information about retreat programme can be obtained from the 'Outreach Office' at the above address.

Children over 12 welcome. Good rail and road connections (M4, Exit 12: 7 miles; local BR station Midgham: served from Paddington). Oxford, Stonehenge and Winchester all within 50 minutes drive.

*SPIRITUAL ORIENTATION:*
*Christian/Catholic.*
*ACCOMMODATION:*
*30 bedspaces in 24 rooms (includes 24 singles); Group B&B; Group full board; Group self-catering; Individual B&B; Individual full board; Individual self catering; No smoking in building; Several small spaces; Venue for hire.*
*EVENT TYPES:*
*Guided group retreats; Guided individual retreats; Self directed retreats.*
*SUITABILITY OR SPECIALISM:*
*Adults; Couples; Families with children; Young people 12 to 18.*
*SUBJECT SPECIALITIES:*
*Meditation; Prayer.*

# Emerson College

Forest Row
East Sussex
RH18 5JX
Telephone: 01342 822238
Facsimile: 01342 826055

Emerson College is an adult centre for training and research based on the work of Rudolf Steiner. Courses are offered in Waldorf teacher training, storytelling, creative writing, sculpture, visual arts and many other themes. Our courses range in length from one day to three years. We run weekend workshops and an annual summer school. Every year we offer an individual retreat from 24 December through to 6 January (inclusive). Please contact the College for further details.

SPIRITUAL ORIENTATION:
Anthroposophical.
ACCOMMODATION:
140 bedspaces in 140 rooms; Large indoor space; No smoking in building; Several small spaces; Special diets.
EVENT TYPES:
Own course programme; Regeneration programmes; Teacher training; Working holidays.
SUITABILITY OR SPECIALISM:
Adults.
SUBJECT SPECIALITIES:
Arts & Crafts; Self expression.

# Equilibrium

Contact: Jeanette McKenzie
The Stable Centre
Little Abshot Road
Titchfield Common, Fareham
Hampshire
PO14 4LN
Telephone: 01489 572451
Facsimile: 01489 572451
E-Mail: 101604.2063@compuserve.com

Have a holiday at Equilibrium and change your life! The Stable Centre provides a beautiful venue with a swimming pool in a lovely rural setting in Hampshire, away from it all where you can detoxify your mind and body, finding balance and spiritual harmony.

We offer personalised retreats including individual transformation sessions for mental and emotional detoxification, bodycare - massage, polarity, integrational bodywork - and a natural living diet. We also offer Polarity Training, Vedic Astrology, acupuncture and meditation.

One to fourteen day programmes available from £85 per day inclusive of room, board and your personal therapy programme. Double and single bedrooms plus dormitories for large workshops.

*ACCOMMODATION:*
*15 bedspaces in 6 rooms (includes 2 singles); Exclusively vegetarian; Individual full board; Large indoor space; No smoking in building; Several small spaces; Special diets.*
*EVENT TYPES:*
*Accredited courses; Guided group retreats; Guided individual retreats; Own course programme; Regeneration programmes; Teacher training.*
*SUBJECT SPECIALITIES:*
*Bodywork & Breathwork; Counselling; Food & Horticulture; Group Process; Health & Healing; Inner process; Meditation.*

# Four Winds Centre ⛵

*High Thicket Road*
*Dockenfield*
*Farnham*
*Surrey*
*GU10 4HE*
*Telephone: 01252 793990*

A residential transpersonal centre in a secluded forest setting 45 miles from London. Available for groups up to 32 people with option of vegetarian catering. We also run summer and winter programmes, and individual retreats can be arranged midweek.

*ACCOMMODATION:*
*26 bedspaces in 8 rooms (includes 1 single); Exclusively vegetarian; Group full board; Group self-catering; Large indoor space; No smoking in building; Special diets; Venue for hire.*
*EVENT TYPES:*
*Own course programme; Guided group retreats; Guided individual retreats; Self-directed retreats; Regeneration programmes.*
*SUITABILITY OR SPECIALISM:*
*Adults; Men; Women.*
*SUBJECT SPECIALITIES:*
*Counselling; Group Process; Health & Healing; Inner process; Meditation; Prayer; Self expression.*

# The Friars

Contact: Margaret Dunk
Aylesford Priory
Aylesford
Kent
ME20 7BX
Telephone: 01622 717272
Facsimile: 01622 715575

Home of a community of Carmelite Friars running a programme of retreats. The guesthouse welcomes individuals and groups. Conferences can also be accommodated.

SPIRITUAL ORIENTATION:
Christian/Catholic.
ACCOMMODATION:
100 bedspaces in 62 rooms (includes 40 singles); Child friendly all ages; Group B&B; Group full board; Individual B&B; Individual full board; Large indoor space; Several small spaces; Special diets; Venue for hire; Wheelchair accessible.
EVENT TYPES:
Guided group retreats; Own course programme; Self directed retreats.
SUITABILITY OR SPECIALISM:
Adults; Men; Women.
SUBJECT SPECIALITIES:
Counselling; Prayer.

# Little Grove

Grove Lane
Orchard Leigh
Chesham
Buckinghamshire
HP5 3QQ
Telephone: 01494 782720
Facsimile: 01494 776066

A venue in the country near the city. Long-established and popular with all kinds of groups. Quiet, beautiful grounds surrounded by farmland. Large airy meeting room and other spaces available, with all visual and audio aids. Excellent catering or DIY if preferred. Sauna.

ACCOMMODATION:
18 bedspaces in 4 rooms; Camping; Child friendly over 5; Group full board; Group self-catering; Large indoor space; Several small spaces; Special diets; Venue for hire; Wheelchair accessible.
EVENT TYPES:
Guided group retreats; Own course programme; Working holidays.
SUITABILITY OR SPECIALISM:
Adults.

# Old Alresford Place

Contact: The Warden
Old Alresford Place
Alresford
Hampshire
SO24 9DH
Telephone: 01962 732518
Facsimile: 01962 732518

Set in the heart of Hampshire. Available for Group or Individual bookings. Fifty bedspaces in twenty-five rooms. A place for retreats, workshops, conferences for self-development and spiritual growth. Also Drop-in Days for quiet and reflection. Good home cooking, friendly and flexible staff. Twenty-four hour and Day rates. Send for a brochure and current price list.

*continued overleaf*

*Old Arlesford Place continued*

**SPIRITUAL ORIENTATION:**
Christian/Protestant.
**ACCOMMODATION:**
50 bedspaces in 25 rooms (includes 5 singles); Child friendly all ages; Group full board; Individual full board; Large indoor space; Several small spaces; Special diets; Venue for hire.
**EVENT TYPES:**
Guided group retreats; Guided individual retreats; Own course programme; Self directed retreats.
**SUITABILITY OR SPECIALISM:**
Adults; Couples; Families with children; Men; Older people; Women.
**SUBJECT SPECIALITIES:**
Counselling; Group Process; Inner process; Meditation; Prayer.

# Redfield Centre ✿

*Redfield*
*Buckingham Road*
*Winslow*
*Buckinghamshire*
*MK18 3LZ*
*Telephone: 01296 714983*
*Facsimile: 01296 714983*

*E-Mail: 106031.2416@compuserve.com*
*World Wide Web: http://ourworld.*
*compuserve.com/homepages/*
*Redfield_Community/redcent.htm*

Accommodation for groups in a peaceful setting halfway between London and Birmingham and convenient for Oxford, Northampton, Milton Keynes and Luton. Residential facilities are located in a self-contained cottage away from the Main House which is occupied by the Redfield Community. 16 people can be accommodated but we have had larger groups by using mattresses on the floor; outlying B&Bs; and (in Summer) camping. Seventeen acre estate includes woodland and tennis court. Groups are usually self-contained but there are possibilities for participating in tasks with members of the Community. Various large meeting spaces available. Special diets catered for within a vegetarian kitchen (self-catering is an option). Groups using the Centre have included: Permaculture designers; Buddhist retreatants; and Peace Brigade International.

ACCOMMODATION:
*16 bedspaces in 5 rooms; Camping; Child friendly all ages; Child minding service; Exclusively vegetarian; Group B&B; Group full board; Group self-catering; Large indoor space; No smoking in building; Several small spaces; Special diets; Venue for hire.*
EVENT TYPES:
*Accredited courses; Own course programme; Working holidays.*
SUBJECT SPECIALITIES:
*Alternative lifestyles & technology; Conservation work; Food & Horticulture; Health & Healing; Outdoor activities.*

# Roydon Hall

*East Peckham
Tonbridge, Kent
TN12 5NH
Telephone: 01622 812121
Facsimile: 01622 813959*

Roydon Hall is a splendid Tudor Manor with many original 16th century features. It has a wonderful peaceful atmosphere and is set in 10 acres of woodlands, lawns, terraces and courtyard, commanding a magnificent view of the Weald of Kent. Single, double, twin and family rooms are available, with or without en-suite facilities. All rooms are centrally heated. Roydon Hall also has a

natural health centre and regularly holds residential meditation courses. Conferences and public events are also catered for. Bed and delicious vegetarian cooked breakfast from £19 per person per night. Less than 1 hour from central London by car or train.

ACCOMMODATION:
*29 bedspaces in 15 rooms (includes 4 singles); Child friendly all ages; Exclusively vegetarian; Group B&B; Group full board; Individual B&B; Large indoor space; No smoking in building; Several small spaces; Special diets; Venue for hire.*
EVENT TYPES:
*Own course programme.*

# Sedlescombe Vineyard

*Contact: Irma Hartman-Cook
Sedlescombe Vineyard
Cripps Corner, Sedlescombe
Robertsbridge, East Sussex
TN32 5SA
Telephone: 01580 830715
Facsimile: 01580 830122*

Situated in the heart of "Cobb Country", England's leading organic vineyard offers a warm welcome and a chance to explore this fascinating region, just a couple of hours' drive from London. Special diets catered for. B&B from £16 per night. Brochure available.

*continued overleaf.*

*Sedlescombe Vineyard continued*

SPIRITUAL ORIENTATION:
*Eco-spirituality.*
ACCOMMODATION:
*6 bedspaces in 2 rooms; Child friendly all ages; Individual B&B; No smoking in building; Special diets.*
EVENT TYPES:
*Working holidays; Couples.*
SUBJECT SPECIALITIES:
*Alternative lifestyles & technology; Food & Horticulture.*

# Stacklands Retreat House

*Contact: Michael Robson*
*Stacklands*
*West Kingsdown*
*Sevenoaks*
*Kent*
*TN15 6AN*
*Telephone: 01474 852247*

Stacklands, the home of the Society of Retreat Conductors, is an Anglican centre for the study and giving of retreats according to the spiritual exercises of St Ignatius Loyola: a series of scripture-based meditations designed to help the retreatant to become more aware of his or her true self; to become more Christ-centred and to respond more fully to God's love. Send a stamped addressed envelope to the Administrator for a programme.

SPIRITUAL ORIENTATION:
*Christian/Catholic.*
ACCOMMODATION:
*20 bedspaces in 20 rooms (includes 20 singles); Group B&B; Group full board; Individual B&B; Individual full board; Several small spaces; Special diets; Wheelchair accessible.*
EVENT TYPES:
*Guided group retreats; Guided individual retreats; Own course programme; Self directed retreats.*
SUITABILITY OR SPECIALISM:
*Adults; Gay men; Lesbian women; Men; Older people; Women.*
SUBJECT SPECIALITIES:
*Counselling; Meditation; Prayer.*

# Turvey Abbey

*Contact: Retreat Secretary*
*Priory of Our Lady of Peace*
*Turvey*
*Bedfordshire*
*MK43 8DE*
*Telephone: 01234 881432*
*Facsimile: 01234 881538*

Roman Catholic double monastery (Benedictine) offers retreats: Private; guided, group; residential; day courses; ecumenical ministry. Thirteen single rooms, home cooking. Day: £25.00; Weekend courses: £65.00.

*SPIRITUAL ORIENTATION:*
*Christian/Catholic.*
*ACCOMMODATION:*
*16 bedspaces in 13 rooms (includes 8 singles); Group B&B; Group full board; Individual B&B; Individual full board; No smoking in building; Several small spaces; Venue for hire.*

*EVENT TYPES:*
*Guided group retreats; Guided individual retreats; Own course programme; Self directed retreats.*
*SUBJECT SPECIALITIES:*
*Arts & Crafts; Inner process; Meditation; Prayer.*

# Woodrow High House

*Contact: Roy Hickman*
*Woodrow High House*
*Cherry Lane*
*Woodrow*
*Amersham*
*Buckinghamshire*
*HP7 0QG*
*Telephone: 01494 433531*
*Facsimile: 01494 431391*

Set in the beautiful Chiltern Hills near Amersham, and in its own 24 acres of grounds this lovely old 17th Century manor house (occupied by Oliver Cromwell's family during the Civil War) provides excellent training and conference facilities. The House is owned by the London Federation of Clubs for Young People but the facilities are available for hire for self-contained groups running residential and day conferences. For brochure and prices please telephone.

*ACCOMMODATION:*
*52 bedspaces in 18 rooms (includes 9 singles); Camping; Child friendly all ages; Group full board; No smoking in building; Special diets; Venue for hire; Wheelchair accessible.*
*SUITABILITY OR SPECIALISM:*
*Adults; Families with children; Men; Women; Young people 12 to 18.*
*SUBJECT SPECIALITIES:*
*Outdoor activities & Sport.*

*Woodrow High House*

*I*n 1035 a cross was found buried on, what is now, St Michael's Hill above Montacute in Somerset. The cross was put on to an ox-drawn cart which was then set loose. Amazingly the ox made its way to Waltham in Essex where a church was founded. The cross displayed mighty powers. It was said that Harold, then brother-in-law to King Edward the Confessor, was healed of paralysis by the Holy Cross. Later as King Harold he determined to build something more worthy than the little church and so Waltham Abbey was created on the same site. Unfortunately the cross was lost during the Middle Ages.

# Greater London

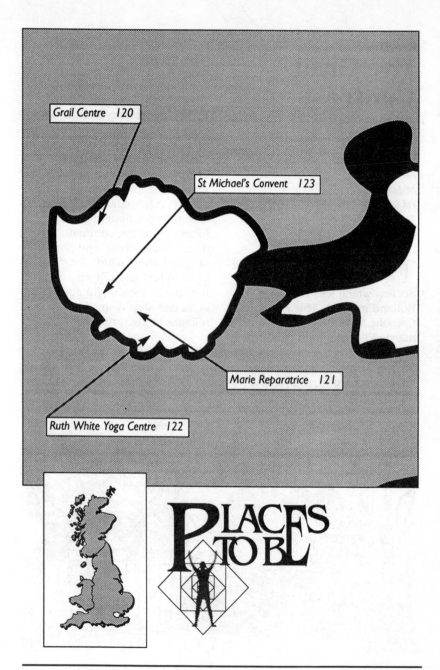

Grail Centre 120

St Michael's Convent 123

Marie Reparatrice 121

Ruth White Yoga Centre 122

PLACES TO BE

# The Grail Centre

*Contact: Diane Kirk*
*The Grail Centre*
*125 Waxwell Lane*
*Pinner*
*Middlesex*
*HA5 3ER*
*Telephone: 0181 866 2195*
*Facsimile: 0181 866 1408*

The Grail Community is one of several branches of the Grail Society which was started in Holland in 1921. This is a Roman Catholic Institute of single and married people, men and women, both young and old. The Society seeks, in an increasingly impersonal world, to promote understanding of the uniqueness and value of each person. The long term community at "Waxwell" consists of women who, choosing to remain single, make a life commitment. The community home is an Elizabethan farmhouse (with library, guest wing and conference extensions) set in ten acres of cultivated and wilderness land. The work of the community includes: support for families and married people; publishing; hospitality; residential courses on arts, religion, human growth, focussing on the spiritual; helping those under stress; and provision of space and solitude for those seeking rest and prayer. Individuals looking for space and quiet can stay in small hermitages in the grounds.

*SPIRITUAL ORIENTATION:*
*Christian/Catholic.*
*ACCOMMODATION:*
*32 bedspaces in 17 rooms, Group full board; Several small spaces; Venue for hire.*
*EVENT TYPES:*
*Own course programme.*

# Marie Reparatrice

Marie Reparatrice Centre
115 Ridgway
Wimbledon
LONDON
SW19 4RB
Telephone: 0181 946 1088
Facsimile: 0181 947 9820

A modern, two storey retreat centre, set in its own grounds, close to Wimbledon Common. We offer retreats, workshops and a place for quiet reflection.

SPIRITUAL ORIENTATION:
Christian/Catholic.
ACCOMMODATION:
28 bedspaces in 28 single rooms; Group full board; Individual B&B; Individual full board; No smoking in building; Several small spaces; Special diets; Venue for hire.
EVENT TYPES:
Guided group retreats; Guided individual retreats; Own course programme; Self directed retreats.
SUITABILITY OR SPECIALISM:
Adults; Men; Women.
SUBJECT SPECIALITIES:
Meditation; Prayer.

# Ruth White Yoga Centre

Church Farm House
Spring Close Lane
Cheam
Surrey
SM3 8PU
Telephone: 0181 644 0309
Facsimile: 0181 644 0309

*ACCOMMODATION:*
*30 bedspaces in 20 rooms; Group full board.*
*EVENT TYPES:*
*Own course programme.*
*SUBJECT SPECIALITIES:*
*Bodywork & Breathwork; Health & Healing.*

Workshops are held throughout the British Isles. All are in quiet country residences with beautiful surroundings and an ambience conducive to yoga. Caring hospitality is offered; delicious and plentiful vegetarian cuisine; comfortable bedrooms and elegant, spacious practice rooms. John and Ruth White, both trained in the Iyengar tradition, now run the Yoga Centre in Cheam. All abilities are welcome from beginners to teachers' training, as Ruth is adept at meeting the ever-changing needs of students. There is no doubt that you will enjoy Ruth's teaching, given with clear precise instruction. Yoga is an excellent form of stress release, much needed today.

# St Michael's Convent

56 Ham Common
Richmond
Surrey
TW10 7JH
Telephone: 0181 940 8711
Facsimile: 0181 332 2927

With its beautiful four acre garden, the Mother House of the Community of the Sisters of the Church (Anglican) near Richmond Park and the River Thames - provides a haven of peace and quiet, yet is only a short journey from Richmond Station (London Underground and British Rail). We offer accommodation to individuals and groups for retreats, quiet days, personal study or simply a time apart for rest and refreshment - as well as organised weekend workshops on such topics as Spirituality and Colour, painting, circle dancing, MBTI ... Our Conference Area may be reserved for day retreats and conferences (groups up to 30: £60 per day.

SPIRITUAL ORIENTATION:
Christian/Anglican.
ACCOMMODATION:
17 bedspaces (includes 15 single rooms), Group full board; Individual B&B; Individual full board; Individual self catering; Large indoor space; No smoking in building; Several small spaces; Special diets; Venue for hire.
EVENT TYPES:
Guided group retreats; Guided individual retreats; Own course programme; Self directed retreats.
SUBJECT SPECIALITIES:
Adults; Men; Women.
SUBJECT SPECIALITIES:
Arts & Crafts; Counselling; Health & Healing; Inner process; Meditation; Prayer; Self expression.

# Multiple Locations and Places outside the United Kingdom

# Head for the Hills

The Recreation Hall
Garth, Builth
Powys
LD4 4AT
Telephone: 01591 620388

Based in Wales, we annually present a sequence of walking adventures throughout Britain. Varying in length from a few days to over a week they offer a rare opportunity to slip out of the modern world into the timelessness of Nature. The party are guided along paths which reach into pre-history while the crew drive the Land Rover and trailer ahead and establish our splendid camp for the night in a wild place specially arranged. Our vegetarian cuisine is famous. Cost: around £30 per night full board. Accommodation: Individual tents, sleeping mats. Cupboards - even a library - in the walk-in trailer. Main tent and all facilities but in nomadic form. Accompanied children welcome over 11 (younger on "St David's").

Contact us, too, for our offshoot "Bootlace" in the Spanish Alpujarra.

*SPIRITUAL ORIENTATION:*
*Attuning to Nature.*
*ACCOMMODATION:*
*12 bedspaces in 12 tents; Camping;*
*Exclusively vegetarian; Individual full board.*
*SUITABILITY OR SPECIALISM:*
*Adults; Accompanied young people 12 to 18.*

# VegiVentures

*Contact: Nigel Walker*
*Castle Cottage, Castle Square*
*Castle Acre*
*Norfolk*
*PE32 2AJ*
*Telephone: 01760 755888*

Holidays and houseparties with great vegetarian/vegan food. Venues include: Crete, Peru, Bali, the English Lake District and Christmas and New Year Celebrations in Wales. Also low cost "Creativity Weekends" in England. All holidays are ideal for single people and couples. Phone for a free brochure.

*PARTICIPANT TYPES:*
*Adults; Couples.*

# France

# Beau Champ

*Montpeyroux*
*Dordogne*
*France*
*F-24610*
*Telephone: 00 33 53 82 69 98*
*Facsimile: 00 33  57 40 65 65*
*E-Mail:  johncant@in-net.inba.fr*

Beau Champ is 8 hectares of woods, meadows and gardens located in the south-west of France. Beau Champ is also a community that works towards creating an ecologically-sound lifestyle. During the summer, we accommodate guests sympathetic to our ideals and looking for low-cost holidays. B&B and full-board is available for groups, families and individuals with dormitory accommodation, camping and a few private rooms. Food is vege-tarian, much coming straight from our organic gardens. Our facilities are simple, including many "alternative technologies" such as reed-beds, composting toilets, and solar water-heating. The house is surrounded by woods, creating a private and tranquil space. 5 km away is a lakeside family resort with swimming, sports, and restau-rants. Please write in advance to arrange accommodation.

SPIRITUAL ORIENTATION:
*Eco-spirituality.*
ACCOMMODATION:
*15 bedspaces in 4 rooms (includes 3 singles); Camping; Child friendly over 5; Child minding service; Exclusively vegetarian; Group B&B; Group full board; Individual B&B; Individual full board; Large indoor space; No smoking in building; Several small spaces; Special diets; Venue for hire.*
EVENT TYPES:
*Working holidays.*
SUBJECT SPECIALITIES:
*Alternative lifestyles & technology; Arts & Crafts; Conservation work; Food & Horticulture.*

# Le Blé en Herbe

*Contact: Maria Sperring*
*Le Blé en Herbe*
*Puissetier*
*La Cellette*
*France*
*F-23350*
*Telephone: 00 33 05 55 80 62 83*

Nestling in the foothills of the Massif Central, Le Blé is a vegetarian guesthouse and small campsite, with 7.5 acres of beautiful organic gardens, field and woods. A haven for wild flowers, butterflies and birds of prey, it's an ideal place for rural retreat. Far from traffic and pollution, relax and recharge your energies embraced by the gentle hum of unspoilt Nature. Welcoming you are Maria Sperring - gardener and masseuse, and Clare Davies -

gourmet cook and craftswoman. We offer B&B, full-board, camping and courses (eg herbalism, massage, voicework). We provide wholefood vegetarian/ vegan meals with organic produce fresh daily from the "Sun" garden. Produce for sale to self-catering campers. Nurture your heart and mind in this peaceful atmosphere, as we care for body and soil. Nearest station is Gueret. 300 miles from Dieppe, Caen and Le Havre. Bookings only, maximum number of guests 15. Summer 1997 rates: B&B 80FF; Full board 160FF; Camping 20FF.

*SPIRITUAL ORIENTATION:*
*Eco-spirituality.*
*ACCOMMODATION:*
*8 bedspaces in 4 rooms (includes 2 singles); Camping; Child friendly all ages; Exclusively vegetarian; Group B&B; Group full board; Individual B&B; Individual full board; Individual self catering; Large indoor space; No smoking in building; Several small spaces; Special diets; Venue for hire.*
*EVENT TYPES:*
*Guided group retreats; Own course programme; Working holidays.*
*SUITABILITY OR SPECIALISM:*
*Adults; Couples; Families with children.*
*SUBJECT SPECIALITIES:*
*Alternative lifestyles & technology; Bodywork & Breathwork; Food & Horticulture; Group Process; Health & Healing; Self expression.*

# Coat-Aillis

Contact: Simon or Paulien Pocock
Coat-Aillis
St Sébastien
Plestin-les-Grèves
FRANCE
F-22310
Telephone: 00 33 96 35 75 51
Facsimile: 00 33 96 35 75 51

A converted Breton farmstead consisting of three gites, a large farmhouse, swimming pool, gardens, cider orchard and converted wooden studio for workshops. Set in the beautiful tranquil countryside, 20 minutes walk through woods to the sea. We are within easy access of Roscoft or St Malo from where we can transport small groups with our own minibus. There are always yoga and shiatsu therapists on site which makes it an ideal venue for workshops or family holidays. Try one of our regular yoga/ walking retreats!

ACCOMMODATION:
30 bedspaces in 15 rooms; Child friendly all ages; Group full board; Venue for hire.
EVENT TYPES:
Own course programme.
SUITABILITY OR SPECIALISM:
Adults; Families with children.
SUBJECT SPECIALITIES:
Bodywork & Breathwork; Health & Healing.

# Domaine de Montfleuri

Contact: Dominique Barron
Domaine de Montfleuri
Bouglon
France
F-47250
Telephone: 00 33 05 53 20 61 30

Welcome to Montfleuri, a handsome 18th Century residence surrounded by gardens with trees and flowers growing in many colourful, fragrant nooks and crannies - standing on a sunny hillside this haven of peace offers panoramic views over the gentle rolling countryside of Lot-et-Garonne.

With Dominique's hospitality, you will enjoy comfortable, bright, spacious bedrooms, delicious vegetarian meals, mostly from home-grown organic vegetables; four acres of gardens; park and orchard in which to relax; the beautiful swimming pool; cheerful logfires in the winter; and sights of interest to tourists. At all seasons, an ideal venue for workshops touching personal development, arts, crafts, nature ...

*SPIRITUAL ORIENTATION:*
*Anthroposophical; Eco-spirituality; Positive thinking.*
*ACCOMMODATION:*
*15 bedspaces in 5 rooms; Child friendly all ages; Exclusively vegetarian; Individual B&B; Large indoor space; No smoking in building; Several small spaces; Venue for hire.*
*SUITABILITY OR SPECIALISM:*
*Adults; Couples; Families with children.*
*SUBJECT SPECIALITIES:*
*Arts & Crafts; Food & Horticulture; Outdoor activities & Sport.*

# Le Plessis Vegetarian Guesthouse

*Contact: Janine & Steve Judges*
*Le Plessis, Plumaudan*
*France*
*F-22350*
*Telephone: 00 33 96 86 00 44*

L e Plessis is a vegetarian haven in the beautiful Breton countryside. At one time a working farm, Le Plessis has been recently renovated to combine the charm of the original rustic features of the farmhouse with modern comfort. The atmosphere is relaxed and friendly, a home away from home.

We are ideally situated for Channel crossings to St Malo, Caen, Cherbourg and Roscoff. Our nearest town, Dinan, is a magnificent mediaeval fortress town overlooking an ancient port on the River Rance.

*continued overleaf*

*Le Plessis continued*

We are also within easy reach of many other places of interest, including Merlin's Tomb and the Fountain of Youth in the Forest of Paimpont, Rennes, megaliths, as well as the vast sandy beaches of the Côte d'Emeraude. Whether walking, cycling or motoring, our region has much to offer.

Excellent vegetarian meals are also on offer. Fresh produce, organic when available, is used to create healthy breakfasts and varied and imaginative three course evening meals, served in generous portions. Whether you stay for two nights or two weeks you will find the food to be of a consistently high standard. We also have a charming self-catering cottage (6 beds in 2 rooms) next door to the guesthouse. Cottage guests are welcome to dine in the guesthouse dining room. Vegans welcome. Reasonable prices. Vegetarian proprietors.

*ACCOMMODATION:*
*14 bedspaces in 5 rooms; Child friendly all ages; Exclusively vegetarian; Group B&B; Group half board; Group self-catering; Individual half board; Individual B&B; Individual self catering.*

# Greece

# Holiday Azogires ⚓

*Contact: Jilly Batchelar*
*153 Carden Avenue*
*Brighton*
*Sussex*
*BN1 8LA*
*Telephone: 01273 564230*

Azogires is a small village, high in the mountains above the beach resort of Paleochora in South West Crete. The road into the village is unmade and the village is unspoilt. The scenery is spectacular.

# Skyros Centre - Atsitsa

We have basic accommodation for 16 people in twin bedded rooms. These are spacious and each has its own shower and separate toilet, plus a balcony with views straight down the valley and out to sea. Look up and you will sometimes see eagles circling, look out and take in the uninterrupted view of trees, mountain and valley. The price of your holiday includes breakfast every morning and five delicious vegetarian evening meals each week. Every week something different happens in Azogires. Our one and two week holidays include discovery trips of South West Crete, Personal Development workshops, walking, painting and much more. Information sheets are available for each holiday. For those who just want to relax, it is possible to come to Azogires and do just that. Ask us for further details.

ACCOMMODATION:
16 bedspaces in 8 rooms, Individual B&B.
EVENT TYPES:
Own course programme.
SUBJECT SPECIALITIES:
Arts & Crafts; Inner process; Outdoor activities & Sport.

Contact: Helen Akif or Rochelle Richards
Skyros Centre
92 Prince of Wales Road
London
NW5 3NE
Telephone: 0171 267 4424
Facsimile: 0171 284 3063
E-Mail: skyros@easynet.co.uk

Holidays for the mind, body and spirit on the beautiful Greek island of Skyros.

*continued overleaf*

*Skyros-Atsitsa continued*

Established for 18 years as the foremost European 'alternative' holiday centre we offer two week sessions ranging from art, creative writing, personal development, t'ai chi, yoga, healing and massage to singing, drumming, dance, laughter, mime and windsurfing. We also specialise in group therapy with world renowned therapists and writer's workshops with famous writers such as Sue Townsend, Andrew Davies and Wendy Cope. We offer delicious food & cater for vegetarians with a friendly community atmosphere in the most beautiful surroundings of the pine forest and sea of Atsitsa and the Skyros village and monastery of the Skyros Centre.

*ACCOMMODATION:*
*160 bedspaces in 80 rooms; Child friendly over 5; Group full board; Individual full board.*
*EVENT TYPES:*
*Accredited courses; Regeneration programmes; Working holidays.*
*SUITABILITY OR SPECIALISM:*
*Adults; Couples; Families with children; Gay men; Lesbian women; Men; Older people; Women; Young people 12 to 18.*
*SUBJECT SPECIALITIES:*
*Alternative lifestyles & technology; Arts & Crafts; Bodywork & Breathwork; Conservation work; Counselling; Group Process; Health & Healing; Inner process; Meditation; Outdoor activities & Sport; Self expression.*

# Ireland

# Chrysalis

*Donard*
*County Wicklow*
*Ireland*
*Telephone: 00 353 45 404713*
*Facsimile: 00 353 45 404713*

A homely holistic centre in West Wicklow (one hour south of Dublin) specialising in residential courses in many aspects of personal growth and spirituality, with facilities for private group bookings. Converted 18th Century rectory and wooden chalet (we're in the process of building a Hermitage in our grounds for individual retreats). Restful rural setting with two welcoming red setter dogs.

Sauna, craft shop, library, organic garden and delicious meals. All this and firm mattresses on the beds! We produce a bi-annual varied programme of events available on request. Look forward to welcoming you to Ireland.

*SPIRITUAL ORIENTATION:*
*Christian/Ecumenical.*
*ACCOMMODATION:*
*24 bedspaces in 10 rooms (includes 3 singles); Exclusively vegetarian; Group full board; Group self-catering; Individual B&B; Individual full board; Individual self catering; Large indoor space; No smoking in building; Several small spaces; Special diets; Venue for hire.*
*EVENT TYPES:*
*Guided group retreats; Own course programme.*
*SUITABILITY OR SPECIALISM:*
*Adults.*
*SUBJECT SPECIALITIES:*
*Bodywork & Breathwork; Counselling; Group Process; Health & Healing; Inner process; Meditation.*

# Italy

# Az Agriturista Montali

*Via Montali 23*
*Tavernelle di Panicale (PG)*
*Italy*
*I-06068*
*Telephone: 00 39 75 8350680*

Country House Montali is located in a beautiful position in Umbria and Tuscany. Situated on a plateau, which dominates the surrounding countryside, there are wonderful views of Trasimeno Lake, Lower Tuscany and the Valley of Perugia.

*continued overleaf*

*Az Agriturista Montali continued*

An old stone farm house - completely restored with traditional materials - welcomes guests in a wonderful and silent peace. Accommodation is in a new building and three rooms have en suite facilities. You can book half or full board. The owners used to run a restaurant and this shows in the delicious recipes perfected over many years. Sometimes there are vegetarian cookery courses. Other possibilities include: a dip in the beautiful swimming pool; a trek in the nearby forest; excursions to Assisi, Gubbio etc; and live evening concerts of world music given by the owners who are passionate musicians.

*ACCOMMODATION:*
*10 bedspaces in 5 rooms; Exclusively vegetarian; Individual B&B; Individual full board.*
*EVENT TYPES:*
*Own course programme.*
*SUBJECT SPECIALITIES:*
*Food & Horticulture.*

# Spain

# Cortijo Romero

*care of Little Grove*
*Grove Lane, Orchard Leigh*
*Chesham, Buckinghamshire*
*HP5 3QQ*
*Telephone: 01494 782720*
*Facsimile: 01494 776066*

Small groups with exclusive use of delightful buildings, gardens and pool set in an 800 year old olive grove, surrounded by the magnificent Alpujarras National Park. Comfortable rooms, all with bath.

ACCOMMODATION:
22 bedspaces in 14 rooms (includes 6 singles); Exclusively vegetarian; Group full board; Individual full board; Large indoor space; No smoking in building; Several small spaces; Special diets; Venue for hire.
EVENT TYPES:
Accredited courses; Guided group retreats; Own course programme; Self directed retreats; Teacher training.
SUITABILITY:
Adults
SUBJECT SPECIALITIES:
Bodywork & Breathwork; Counselling; Group Process; Health & Healing; Inner process; Meditation; Ritual & Shamanic; Self expression.

---

# Garden of Light

Contact: Tom or Lourdes
El Jardin de Luz
Apto 1126
Ibiza
SPAIN
E-07800
Telephone: 00 34 71 33 46 44
Facsimile: 00 34 71 39 10 86

S ituated between two worlds - Europe and Africa, rising out of the crystal clear waters of the Mediterranean sea, lies the magic island of Ibiza. In the north of the island, secluded among indigenous forests and exotic gardens, El Jardin de Luz offers a beautiful and peaceful setting for residential seminars and workshops. The Centre features a group room which is light and well-equipped; large terraces for working in the open-air; pure drinking water from a natural spring; and serves delicious vegetarian meals with an oriental touch. The sunny and warm climate will enchant you, as will the beautiful sandy beaches, which can be found within walking distance of the Centre.

SPIRITUAL ORIENTATION:
New Age.
ACCOMMODATION:
30 bedspaces in 6 rooms; Exclusively vegetarian; Group full board; Large indoor space; No smoking in building; Venue for hire.
SUITABILITY:
Adults.

# Sunseed Desert Technology

Contact: Margaret & Alex Godden
Sunseed Desert Technology
care of
97b Divinity Road
Oxford
OX4 1LN
Telephone: 01865 721530
Facsimile: 01480 411784

Research, education and eco-logical living are uniquely combined at our research centre in a Spanish village (an hour's walk from the nearest town). We are a project for desert reclamation helping those in poverty on the desert margins with new technologies and new botanical methods. It's possible to join us as a part-time working visitor or a full-time volunteer paying between £50 and £100 per week. Our accommodation is very basic with rooms shared by up to six people; squat latrines; and washing water at the bottom of the hill! But the valley is beautiful; the stars at night are amzing; and there is often a nightingale. Social life centres on conversation, lazing by (or in) the village stream. We'll welcome your curiousity, kindness, ideas, and courage - and we hope that like many of our visitors you'll find these qualities in our project.

ACCOMMODATION:
Child friendly over 5; Exclusively vegetarian; Individual full board.
EVENT TYPES:
Working holidays.
SUITABILITY OR SPECIALISM:
Adults; Families with children.
SUBJECT SPECIALITIES:
Food & Horticulture.

# Turkey

# Huzur Vadisi

care of 3 Crown Place
Aberarth
Aberaeron
Ceredigion
SA46 0LL
Telephone: 01545 570742
Facsimile: 01545 570742

Situated in a beautiful pine forested mountain valley, half an hour from Turkey's Mediterranean coast, Huzur Vadisi is a restored farmhouse set amidst olive and fig groves. Accommodation is in traditional Turkic yurts, spacious, light, and comfortably furnished. Immersed in nature, the only thing to disturb the peace is the hum of the cicadas and the call of the owls. A unique place to experience traditional Turkey, combined with the opprtunity to participate in one of our holistic or creative courses - or to simply take a relaxing holiday to refresh body, mind and spirit in congenial company. Swimming pool.

*ACCOMMODATION:*
*20 bedspaces in 7 rooms; Child friendly over 5; Group full board; Individual full board; No smoking in building; Several small spaces; Venue for hire.*
*EVENT TYPES:*
*Own course programme.*
*SUBJECT SPECIALITIES:*
*Arts & Crafts; Bodywork & Breathwork; Meditation; Self expression.*

# The Bed & Breakfast Seeker's Index

The B&B Seeker's Index is fairly self-explanatory. The entries listed have all said that they offer bed and breakfast and/or full board to individuals. However, standards may vary enormously and will range from conventional (and often) salubrious tourist board recommended venues to very unconventional intentional communities that offer a B&B option to visitors as one way of giving a short-term taste of their lifestyle. So please phone ahead, not only to check on availability but also to make sure that you know exactly what you're going to.

**Vegtn** means that the establishment say they are exclusively vegetarian - but of course they may well cater for more restrictive **Special Diets** within that basic parameter.

**No smoking** is fairly obvious.

**Children over 5** and **Children under 5** refer to the suitability of the venue to children in those age ranges. A very few places have said that they can offer a **Children Minding** service but don't expect this to be available on demand.

**Whlchr Access** refers to accessibility to wheelchairs.

| page number | venue | Individ B&B | Individ full board | Vegtn | No Smokng | Special Diets | Children over 5 | Children under 5 | Child Minding | Wlchr Access |
|---|---|---|---|---|---|---|---|---|---|---|
| | **Scotland** | | | | | | | | | |
| 14 | The Dyemill | ◆ | ◆ | | | ◆ | | ◆ | | |
| 19 | Minton House | ◆ | ◆ | ◆ | ◆ | | ◆ | ◆ | | ◆ |
| 20 | Rhanich Farm | ◆ | ◆ | ◆ | ◆ | | | | | |
| 21 | Talamh | ◆ | | ◆ | | | | | | |
| 23 | Woodwick House | ◆ | ◆ | | | ◆ | ◆ | ◆ | | ◆ |
| | **N & NW England** | | | | | | | | | |
| 27 | Dobroyd Castle | ◆ | ◆ | ◆ | ◆ | | | | | |
| 27 | Loyola Hall | ◆ | ◆ | | | ◆ | | | | ◆ |
| | **Yorkshire & Humberside** | | | | | | | | | |
| 32 | Amadeus | ◆ | ◆ | ◆ | ◆ | ◆ | | ◆ | | |
| 34 | Prospect Cottage | ◆ | | ◆ | ◆ | | ◆ | ◆ | | |
| 34 | Sansbury Place | ◆ | | ◆ | | ◆ | ◆ | | | |
| 35 | Wydale Hall | ◆ | | | | | | | | |
| | **East Anglia** | | | | | | | | | |
| 39 | Bowthorpe Com Trust | ◆ | | | | | | | | |
| 39 | Castle Cottage | ◆ | | ◆ | | | | | | |
| 41 | Old Red Lion | ◆ | ◆ | ◆ | ◆ | ◆ | ◆ | ◆ | | |
| 42 | Old Stable House Centre | ◆ | | | ◆ | ◆ | | | | ◆ |

| page number | venue | Individ B&B | Individ full board | Vegtn | No Smokng | Special Diets | Children over 5 | Children under 5 | Child Minding | Wlchr Access |
|---|---|---|---|---|---|---|---|---|---|---|
| 43 | Rumwood | ✦ | ✦ | | ✦ | ✦ | | | | |
| 44 | Wood Norton Hall | ✦ | | ✦ | ✦ | ✦ | | | | |
| | **East Midlands** | | | | | | | | | |
| 49 | New House Farm | ✦ | | | ✦ | ✦ | ✦ | ✦ | ✦ | |
| | **West Midlands** | | | | | | | | | |
| 54 | Canon Frome | ✦ | | | | | ✦ | ✦ | | |
| 56 | The Grange | ✦ | ✦ | | ✦ | ✦ | | | | ✦ |
| 58 | Runnings Park | ✦ | ✦ | | ✦ | ✦ | | | | |
| | **Wales** | | | | | | | | | |
| 63 | Graig Fach | ✦ | ✦ | | ✦ | ✦ | ✦ | ✦ | ✦ | |
| 66 | Talbontdrain | ✦ | ✦ | | ✦ | | | | | |
| 67 | Treiorwg Organic Farm | ✦ | ✦ | | ✦ | | | | | |
| 68 | Trigonos Centre | ✦ | ✦ | | ✦ | ✦ | ✦ | ✦ | | ✦ |
| 69 | West Usk Lighthouse | ✦ | | | ✦ | ✦ | ✦ | ✦ | | |
| 70 | Wilderness Trust | ✦ | ✦ | | ✦ | ✦ | ✦ | ✦ | | |
| | **South West England** | | | | | | | | | |
| 101 | Ashburton Centre | ✦ | ✦ | ✦ | ✦ | ✦ | | | | |
| 75 | Beacon Centre | ✦ | | | ✦ | ✦ | ✦ | ✦ | | |
| 76 | Beech Hill | ✦ | | ✦ | | ✦ | | | | ✦ |

| # | Name | 1 | 2 | 3 | 4 | 5 | 6 | 7 | 8 | 9 | 10 | 11 | 12 | 13 | 14 | 15 | 16 | 17 | 18 | 19 | 20 | 21 |
|---|------|---|---|---|---|---|---|---|---|---|----|----|----|----|----|----|----|----|----|----|----|----|
| 76 | Boswednack Manor | | | | | | | ◆ | ◆ | | | | | | | | | ◆ | | | | |
| 77 | C A E R | ◆ | ◆ | ◆ | ◆ | ◆ | | ◆ | ◆ | ◆ | ◆ | ◆ | ◆ | ◆ | ◆ | | ◆ | ◆ | | | ◆ | ◆ |
| 79 | Exmoor Lodge | | | ◆ | | | | | ◆ | ◆ | ◆ | ◆ | | ◆ | ◆ | | | ◆ | | | | |
| 80 | Hawkwood | ◆ | | ◆ | | | | | ◆ | ◆ | | | | ◆ | ◆ | | | | | | | |
| 82 | Hazelwood | | | ◆ | | | | | | ◆ | | | | | | | | | | | | |
| 83 | Little Ash Eco-Farm | | | | ◆ | | | | | ◆ | | | | | | | | | | | | |
| 84 | Merefield House | | | | | | | | ◆ | ◆ | | | | | | | | | | | | |
| 90 | Poplar Herb Farm | | | | | | | ◆ | ◆ | ◆ | | | | | | | | | | | | |
| 92 | Self Realization Centre | ◆ | ◆ | ◆ | | | ◆ | ◆ | ◆ | ◆ | | | | ◆ | | | | | | | | |
| 93 | Shambhala | ◆ | ◆ | ◆ | | | ◆ | ◆ | ◆ | ◆ | | | | ◆ | | | | | | | | |
| 94 | Tidicombe House | | | ◆ | | | | | ◆ | ◆ | | | | | | | | | | | | |
| 96 | Tordown | ◆ | ◆ | ◆ | | | ◆ | ◆ | ◆ | ◆ | | | | | | | | | | | | |
| 97 | Tregeraint House | ◆ | ◆ | ◆ | | | ◆ | ◆ | ◆ | ◆ | | | | | | | | | | | | |
| 97 | Waterfall Cottage | | | ◆ | | | | ◆ | ◆ | ◆ | | | | | | | | | | | | |
| 98 | Wild Pear Centre | | | ◆ | | | | | ◆ | ◆ | | | | | | | | | | | | |
| 100 | Yeo Cottage | | | | | | | | ◆ | ◆ | ◆ | | | | | | | | | | | |
| 100 | Yew Tree Cottage | | ◆ | ◆ | | | | ◆ | ◆ | ◆ | | | | | | | | | | | | |
| | **South East England** | | | | | | | | | | | | | | | | | | | | | |
| 104 | The Abbey | ◆ | | | | | | | ◆ | ◆ | | | | ◆ | | | | ◆ | | | | |
| 105 | Braziers | | | | | | | ◆ | ◆ | ◆ | | | | ◆ | | | | ◆ | | | | |
| 105 | Cherwell Centre | | | | | | | ◆ | ◆ | ◆ | | | | ◆ | | | | ◆ | | | | |

## B&B Seeker's Index

| page number | venue | Individ B&B | Individ full board | Vegtn | No Smokng | Special Diets | Children over 5 | Children under 5 | Child Minding | Wlchr Access |
|---|---|---|---|---|---|---|---|---|---|---|
| 106 | Commonwork | ✦ | | | ✦ | ✦ | | ✦ | | ✦ |
| 107 | Douai Abbey | ✦ | ✦ | | ✦ | | | | | |
| 110 | The Friars | ✦ | ✦ | | | ✦ | ✦ | ✦ | | ✦ |
| 113 | Roydon Hall | ✦ | | ✦ | ✦ | | ✦ | ✦ | | |
| 113 | Sedlescombe Vineyard | ✦ | | | ✦ | ✦ | ✦ | ✦ | | |
| 114 | Stacklands | ✦ | ✦ | | | ✦ | | | | ✦ |
| 115 | Turvey Abbey | ✦ | ✦ | | ✦ | | | | | |
| | **Greater London** | | | | | | | | | |
| 121 | Marie Reparatrice | ✦ | ✦ | | ✦ | ✦ | | | | |
| 123 | St Michael's Convent | ✦ | ✦ | | ✦ | ✦ | | | | |
| | **Outside the UK** | | | | | | | | | |
| 133 | Az Agr Montali | ✦ | ✦ | ✦ | | | | | | |
| 126 | Beau Champ | ✦ | ✦ | ✦ | ✦ | ✦ | ✦ | | | |
| 132 | Chrysalis | ✦ | ✦ | ✦ | ✦ | ✦ | | | | |
| 128 | Dom de Montfleuri | ✦ | ✦ | ✦ | ✦ | | ✦ | ✦ | | |
| 130 | Holiday Azogires | ✦ | | | | | | | | |
| 127 | Le Blé en Herbe | ✦ | ✦ | ✦ | ✦ | ✦ | ✦ | ✦ | | |
| 129 | Le Plessis | ✦ | | ✦ | | | ✦ | ✦ | | |

# The Retreat Seeker's Index

This is the index for you if you're looking for a retreat. Of primary concern to you will probably be whether the venue adheres to a particular faith or has a particular spiritual orientation. For this reason the different places appear in the index grouped according to their affiliations. First up come the places that have no particular orientation or welcome people from all faiths. Christian retreat houses of all types are grouped together but you will find more specific classifications (if these are important) in the regional section.

*Group* means that they offer guided retreats for groups; *Individ* means guided retreats for individuals; *Self D* generally means that a supportive environment is provided for people who are directing their own retreats.

*Progs* refers to the availability of Regeneration Programmes to assist people who are coming out of some kind of crisis.

*Medit* and *Prayer* means that instruction in meditation and prayer are amongst the specialities on offer.

*Whlchr* means wheelchair accessible.

| page | Venue | Region | Group | Individ | Self D | Progs | Medit | Prayer | Wlchr |
|---|---|---|---|---|---|---|---|---|---|
| 17 | Jenny's Bothy | Scotland | ◆ | | ◆ | ◆ | | | |
| 21 | Talamh | Scotland | | | ◆ | | | | |
| 26 | Burnlaw | N & NW England | ◆ | ◆ | ◆ | | ◆ | ◆ | |
| 28 | Oakdene | N & NW England | | | ◆ | | | | |
| 32 | Confluence Centre | Yorkshire & Humberside | | ◆ | ◆ | | | | ◆ |
| 33 | Mountain Hall | Yorkshire & Humberside | ◆ | ◆ | ◆ | ◆ | ◆ | ◆ | ◆ |
| 42 | Old Stable House | East Anglia | ◆ | ◆ | ◆ | | ◆ | ◆ | |
| 43 | Rumwood | East Anglia | ◆ | | ◆ | ◆ | | | |
| 39 | Bowthorpe Com Trust | East Anglia | | | ◆ | | | | |
| 39 | Castle Cottage | East Anglia | | | ◆ | | | | |
| 41 | Old Red Lion | East Anglia | | | ◆ | | | | |
| 50 | White Edge Lodge | East Midlands | | | | | | | |
| 56 | The Grange | West Midlands | ◆ | | ◆ | ◆ | ◆ | | |
| 58 | Runnings Park | West Midlands | ◆ | | ◆ | | | | |
| 57 | Poulstone Court | West Midlands | | | | ◆ | | | |
| 62 | Dyfed PC Farm Trust | Wales | ◆ | ◆ | ◆ | ◆ | | | |
| 66 | Spirit Horse Camps | Wales | ◆ | | | | | ◆ | |
| 63 | Graig Fach | Wales | | ◆ | | | ◆ | | |
| 65 | Penquoit Centre | Wales | | | ◆ | | ◆ | | |
| 77 | C A E R | South West England | ◆ | | ◆ | ◆ | ◆ | | ◆ |

# Retreat Seeker's Index

| page | Venue | Region | Group | Individ | Self D | Progs | Medit | Prayer | Wlchr |
|---|---|---|---|---|---|---|---|---|---|
| 108 | Emerson College | South East England | | | | ♦ | | | |
| | **Buddhist** | | | | | | | | |
| 27 | Dobroyd Castle | N & NW England | ♦ | | | | | | |
| 76 | Boswednack Manor | South West England | | | ♦ | | ♦ | | |
| 58 | Taraloka | West Midlands | ♦ | | | | ♦ | | |
| | **Celtic/Pagan** | | | | | | | | |
| 55 | Earthworm | West Midlands | | | ♦ | | | | |
| 87 | Old Boswednack Farm | South West England | ♦ | | | | | | |
| | **Christian** | | | | | | | | |
| 27 | Loyola Hall | N & NW England | ♦ | ♦ | ♦ | | ♦ | ♦ | ♦ |
| 38 | All Hallows | East Anglia | ♦ | ♦ | ♦ | | | | |
| 105 | Cherwell Centre | South East England | ♦ | ♦ | ♦ | ♦ | ♦ | ♦ | |
| 107 | Douai Abbey | South East England | ♦ | ♦ | ♦ | | ♦ | ♦ | |
| 110 | The Friars | South East England | ♦ | ♦ | ♦ | | ♦ | ♦ | ♦ |
| 114 | Stacklands | South East England | ♦ | ♦ | ♦ | | ♦ | ♦ | ♦ |
| 115 | Turvey Abbey | South East England | ♦ | ♦ | ♦ | | ♦ | ♦ | |
| 121 | Marie Reparatrice | Greater London | ♦ | ♦ | ♦ | | ♦ | ♦ | |
| 132 | Chrysalis | Outside the UK | | | ♦ | | ♦ | | |
| 14 | Carberry | Scotland | | | | | | ♦ | |
| 35 | Wydale Hall | Yorkshire & Humberside | | ♦ | | ♦ | | | |

| No. | Name | Region |
|---|---|---|
| 49 | New House Farm | East Midlands |
| 70 | Wilderness Trust | Wales |
| 88 | Holton Lee | South West England |
| 94 | Sheldon Centre | South West England |
| 111 | Old Alresford | South East England |
| 123 | St Michael's Convent | Greater London |
| | **Eco-spirituality** | |
| 74 | Acorn Centre | South West England |
| 101 | Ashburton Centre | South West England |
| 78 | EarthSpirit | South West England |
| 127 | Le Blé en Herbe | Outside the UK |
| | **New Age** | |
| 44 | Wood Norton Hall | East Anglia |
| 48 | Atlow Mill | East Midlands |
| 50 | Unstone Grange | East Midlands |
| 75 | Beacon Centre | South West England |
| 93 | Shambhala Centre | South West England |
| 97 | Waterfall Cottage | South West England |
| 100 | Yeo Cottage | South West England |
| | **Sufi** | |
| 19 | Minton House | Scotland |

The Venue Seeker's Index should be your first stop if you are a course facilitator or organiser looking for a place to run a workshop. Venues are listed in ascending order of number of bedspaces (**beds**) followed by the number of rooms (**rooms**). Numbers of single rooms are shown in entries in the regional section. Everyone wants information about price but there are so many possible combinations that I've decided to restrict it to the "per person full board per 24 hour hiring out rate". In the **rate** column you'll find letters which correspond to the following ranges:

**A** £25 or less per 24 hours
**B** £25.01 to £35 per 24 hours
**C** £35.01 to £45 per 24 hours
**D** £45.01 or more per 24 hours

**Group B&B**, **Group FB**, **Group SC**, refer to bed and breakfast, full board and self catering for groups. **Camp** means that camping is a possibility.

**Large Space** usually mean that there is at least one large space available to the group and **Small spaces** that several smaller spaces may be on offer.

**Whlchr Access** means wheelchair accessible and **No smking** and **Special Diets** are fairly self explanatory.

# The Venue Seeker's Index

| page number | Venue | Region | bedrooms | rate | Group B&B | Group FB | Group SC | Camp | No Smking | Special Diets | Wchr Access | Large Space spaces | Small spaces |
|---|---|---|---|---|---|---|---|---|---|---|---|---|---|
| 62 | Dyfed PC Farm Trust | Wales | | | | | | ◆ | | | | | |
| **up to 10 bedspaces** | | | | | | | | | | | | | |
| 99 | Yarner Trust | SW Eng | 5 | 3 | A | ◆ | | ◆ | ◆ | | | ◆ | ◆ |
| 14 | The Dyemill | Scotland | 7 | 4 | A | ◆ | ◆ | ◆ | ◆ | | ◆ | ◆ | ◆ |
| 17 | Fossil Bothy | Scotland | 8 | 2 | | | | ◆ | | | | | |
| 127 | Le Blé en Herbe | Non UK | 8 | 4 | A | ◆ | ◆ | | ◆ | ◆ | ◆ | | ◆ | ◆ |
| 97 | Tregeraint House | SW Eng | 8 | 4 | B | ◆ | | | | ◆ | ◆ | | |
| 79 | Exmoor Lodge | SW Eng | 9 | 5 | B | ◆ | ◆ | | | | ◆ | | | |
| 17 | Jenny's Bothy | Scotland | 10 | 2 | | | | ◆ | ◆ | | | | | ◆ |
| 74 | Acorn Centre | SW Eng | 10 | 3 | A | ◆ | ◆ | ◆ | ◆ | ◆ | | | ◆ | |
| 69 | West Usk Lighthouse | Wales | 10 | 6 | D | ◆ | | | | ◆ | | | | |
| **11 to 20 bedspaces** | | | | | | | | | | | | | |
| 88 | Holton Lee | SW Eng | 11 | 7 | C | | ◆ | | | ◆ | ◆ | ◆ | | ◆ |
| 87 | Old Boswednack Farm | SW Eng | 12 | | | | | ◆ | ◆ | ◆ | | | | |
| 50 | White Edge Lodge | E Mid | 12 | 3 | | | | ◆ | | | | | ◆ | |
| 54 | Berrington Hall | W Mid | 12 | 3 | | | | ◆ | ◆ | ◆ | | | ◆ | |
| 70 | Wilderness Trust | Wales | 12 | 5 | | | | ◆ | ◆ | ◆ | ◆ | | ◆ | ◆ |
| 21 | Talamh | Scot | 14 | 3 | | | | | ◆ | | | | ◆ | |
| 32 | Confluence Centre | Yorks | 14 | 5 | C | ◆ | ◆ | ◆ | | ◆ | ◆ | | ◆ | |

| page number | Venue | Region | bedrooms | rate | Group B&B | Group FB | Group SC | Camp | No Smking | Special Diets | Wlchr Access | Large Space | Small spaces |
|---|---|---|---|---|---|---|---|---|---|---|---|---|---|
| 42 | Old Stable House | E Ang | 14 | 9 | B | ♦ | ♦ | ♦ | | ♦ | ♦ | | ♦ | ♦ |
| 104 | The Abbey | SE Eng | 14 | 9 | B | | ♦ | ♦ | | ♦ | | ♦ | ♦ | ♦ |
| 71 | Y Beudy | Wales | 15 | 2 | | | | ♦ | | | | | ♦ | |
| 55 | Earthworm | W Mid | 15 | 3 | A | ♦ | ♦ | | ♦ | ♦ | ♦ | | ♦ | ♦ |
| 126 | Beau Champ | Non UK | 15 | 4 | A | ♦ | ♦ | | ♦ | ♦ | ♦ | | ♦ | ♦ |
| 128 | Dom de Montfleuri | Non UK | 15 | 5 | | | | | | ♦ | | | ♦ | ♦ |
| 49 | New House Farm | E Mid | 15 | 6 | A | ♦ | | | | ♦ | ♦ | | ♦ | ♦ |
| 96 | Tordown | SW Eng | 15 | 7 | | ♦ | | | | | | | ♦ | |
| 40 | Green Wood Centre | E Ang | 15 | 8 | A | | ♦ | | ♦ | ♦ | ♦ | | ♦ | ♦ |
| 85 | Mickleton House | SW Eng | 15 | 10 | B | ♦ | ♦ | | | ♦ | | | ♦ | |
| 29 | Red Water Centre | N Eng | 16 | 5 | B | ♦ | ♦ | ♦ | | ♦ | | | ♦ | ♦ |
| 112 | Redfield Centre | SE Eng | 16 | 5 | A | ♦ | ♦ | ♦ | ♦ | ♦ | ♦ | | ♦ | ♦ |
| 89 | Pelican Centre | SW Eng | 16 | 10 | C | ♦ | ♦ | ♦ | ♦ | | ♦ | | ♦ | ♦ |
| 115 | Turvey Abbey | SE Eng | 16 | 13 | A | ♦ | ♦ | | | ♦ | | | ♦ | |
| 78 | East Down Centre | SW Eng | 17 | 5 | B | ♦ | ♦ | ♦ | | | | | | |
| 123 | St Michael's Convent | Lond | 17 | 15 | A | | ♦ | | ♦ | ♦ | ♦ | | ♦ | ♦ |
| 111 | Little Grove | SE Eng | 18 | 4 | A | | ♦ | ♦ | | | ♦ | ♦ | ♦ | ♦ |
| 19 | Minton House | Scot | 18 | 8 | B | ♦ | ♦ | | | ♦ | | ♦ | ♦ | ♦ |
| 23 | Woodwick House | Scot | 18 | 9 | B | ♦ | ♦ | | | | ♦ | ♦ | ♦ | |

| | Venue | | | | |
|---|---|---|---|---|---|
| 28 | Oakdene | N Eng | 18 | 10 | B |
| 105 | Braziers | SE Eng | 19 | 13 | D |
| 38 | Alpheton Hostel | E Ang | 20 | 3 | |
| 41 | Old Red Lion | E Ang | 20 | 5 | A |
| 76 | Beech Hill | SW Eng | 20 | 5 | B |
| 137 | Huzur Vadisi | Non UK | 20 | 7 | B |
| 101 | Ashburton Centre | SW Eng | 20 | 8 | B |
| **21 to 30 bedspaces** | | | | | |
| 78 | EarthSpirit | SW Eng | 21 | 7 | A |
| 44 | Wood Norton Hall | E Ang | 22 | 8 | A |
| 33 | Mountain Hall | Yorks | 22 | 13 | B |
| 134 | Cortijo Romero | Non UK | 22 | 14 | D |
| 48 | Atlow Mill | E Mid | 23 | 7 | C |
| 62 | Cerridwen | Wales | 23 | 9 | B |
| 132 | Chrysalis | Non UK | 24 | 10 | B |
| 77 | C A E R | SW Eng | 24 | 10 | B |
| 98 | Wild Pear Centre | SW Eng | 25 | 8 | A |
| 58 | Runnings Park | W Mid | 25 | 22 | C |
| 109 | Four Winds | SE Eng | 26 | 8 | B |
| 68 | Trigonos Centre | Wales | 28 | 8 | B |
| 54 | Canon Frome | W Mid | 28 | 14 | |

| page number | Venue | Region | beds | rooms | rate | Group B&B | Group FB | Group SC | Camp | No Smking | Special Diets | Wlchr Access | Large Space | Small spaces |
|---|---|---|---|---|---|---|---|---|---|---|---|---|---|---|
| 121 | Marie Reparatrice | Lond | 28 | 28 | B | | ◆ | | | ◆ | ◆ | | | ◆ |
| 113 | Roydon Hall | SE Eng | 29 | 15 | C | ◆ | | | | ◆ | | | ◆ | ◆ |
| 105 | Cherwell Centre | SE Eng | 29 | 21 | B | ◆ | ◆ | | | ◆ | ◆ | | ◆ | ◆ |
| 65 | Penquoit Centre | Wales | 30 | 2 | A | | ◆ | ◆ | | | | | ◆ | |
| 40 | Chapel Retreat | E Ang | 30 | 6 | | | | ◆ | ◆ | | | | | |
| 135 | Garden of Light | Non UK | 30 | 6 | A | ◆ | ◆ | | | ◆ | | | ◆ | |
| 75 | Beacon Centre | SW Eng | 30 | 12 | A | ◆ | ◆ | ◆ | | ◆ | ◆ | | ◆ | ◆ |
| 128 | Coat-Aillis | Non UK | 30 | 15 | | | ◆ | | | | | | | |
| 56 | The Grange | W Mid | 30 | 17 | B | ◆ | ◆ | | | ◆ | ◆ | ◆ | ◆ | ◆ |
| 107 | Douai Abbey | SE Eng | 30 | 24 | A | ◆ | ◆ | ◆ | | ◆ | | | | ◆ |
| **31 to 60 bedspaces** | | | | | | | | | | | | | | |
| 50 | Unstone Grange | E Mid | 32 | 10 | B | ◆ | ◆ | | ◆ | | ◆ | | ◆ | ◆ |
| 120 | Grail Centre | Lond | 32 | 17 | | | ◆ | | | | | | | ◆ |
| 57 | Poulstone Court | W Mid | 33 | 12 | B | | ◆ | | | | | | ◆ | |
| 86 | Monkton Wyld | SW Eng | 34 | 11 | A | | ◆ | | | ◆ | ◆ | | | |
| 64 | Pen Rhiw | Wales | 34 | 22 | B | ◆ | ◆ | | | ◆ | ◆ | ◆ | ◆ | ◆ |
| 84 | Magdalen Farm | SW Eng | 35 | 8 | A | | ◆ | ◆ | ◆ | ◆ | | ◆ | ◆ | |
| 80 | Grimstone | SW Eng | 40 | 13 | B | | | | | | ◆ | | ◆ | |
| 83 | Lower Shaw Farm | SW Eng | 40 | 15 | | | ◆ | | | | | | ◆ | |

| Page | Venue | Region | | | Grade |
|------|-------|--------|---|---|-------|
| 94 | Sheldon Centre | SW Eng | 50 | 18 | |
| 111 | Old Alresford | SE Eng | 50 | 25 | B |
| 106 | Commonwork | SE Eng | 50 | 27 | D |
| 27 | Loyola Hall | NEng | 50 | 47 | B |
| 115 | Woodrow High Hse | SE Eng | 52 | 18 | B |
| 80 | Hawkwood | SW Eng | 52 | 32 | C |
| **61 or more bedspaces** | | | | | |
| 22 | Woodhall Events | Scot | 67 | 11 | A |
| 35 | Wydale Hall | Yorks | 67 | 34 | |
| 66 | Spirit Horse Camps | Wales | 85 | 13 | A |
| 14 | Carberry | Scot | 90 | 40 | B |
| 110 | The Friars | SE Eng | 100 | 62 | B |
| 110 | All Hallows | E Ang | 120 | 59 | A |

The types of places listed in this book are (quite rightly) very resistant to classification. However, for the book to be useful a degree of classification is necessary. Look the codes below up in this index to find places that offer courses and workshops in these broad subject areas:

**S1** Arts & Crafts
**S2** Self expression
**S3** Bodywork & Breathwork
**S4** Health & Healing
**S5** Outdoor activities & Sport
**S6** Conservation work
**S7** Food & Horticulture
**S8** Altve. lifestyles & technology
**S9** Counselling
**S10** Inner process
**S11** Group process
**S12** Ritual & Shamanic
**S13** Earth mysteries
**S14** Meditation
**S15** Prayer

**Work** means that they can sometimes offer working holidays to people. **Acc** means that some of the courses on offer carry accreditation.

# The Workshop Seeker's Index

| page | Venue | S1 | S2 | S3 | S4 | S5 | S6 | S7 | S8 | S9 | S10 | S11 | S12 | S13 | S14 | S15 | work | acc |
|---|---|---|---|---|---|---|---|---|---|---|---|---|---|---|---|---|---|---|
| | **Scotland** | | | | | | | | | | | | | | | | | |
| 15 | Isle of Erraid | | | | | | | | | | | | | | | | ♦ | |
| 16 | Findhorn | | ♦ | ♦ | ♦ | | | | ♦ | | ♦ | | | | ♦ | | | |
| 19 | Minton House | | | ♦ | ♦ | | | | | | ♦ | | | | ♦ | ♦ | | |
| 20 | Rhanich Farm | | | | | | | ♦ | ♦ | | | | | | | | ♦ | |
| 21 | Talamh | ♦ | ♦ | | ♦ | ♦ | ♦ | ♦ | ♦ | | | | ♦ | | ♦ | | ♦ | |
| | **N & NW England** | | | | | | | | | | | | | | | | | |
| 26 | Burnlaw | ♦ | | | ♦ | | ♦ | ♦ | | | | | | | ♦ | ♦ | ♦ | |
| 27 | Dobroyd Castle | | | | | | | | | | | | | | ♦ | | ♦ | |

| 27 | Loyola Hall |
| 29 | Red Water Centre |
| | **Yorkshire & Humberside** |
| 32 | Confluence Centre |
| 33 | Mountain Hall |
| | **East Anglia** |
| 40 | Green Wood Centre |
| 42 | Old Stable House |
| 43 | Rumwood |
| 44 | Wood Norton Hall |
| | **East Midlands** |
| 48 | Atlow Mill |
| 49 | New House Farm |
| 50 | Unstone Grange |
| | **West Midlands** |
| 54 | Berrington Hall |
| 55 | Earthworm |
| 56 | The Grange |
| 58 | Runnings Park |
| | **Wales** |
| 62 | Dyfed PC Farm Trust |

| page | Venue | S1 | S2 | S3 | S4 | S5 | S6 | S7 | S8 | S9 | S10 | S11 | S12 | S13 | S14 | S15 | work acc |
|------|-------|----|----|----|----|----|----|----|----|----|-----|-----|-----|-----|-----|-----|----------|
| 65 | Penquoit Centre | ♦ | ♦ |  |  |  |  | ♦ |  |  |  |  |  |  | ♦ |  | ♦ |
| 66 | Spirit Horse Camps |  | ♦ | ♦ | ♦ |  |  |  |  | ♦ | ♦ | ♦ | ♦ | ♦ | ♦ | ♦ |  |
| 66 | Talbontdrain |  |  |  |  |  |  | ♦ |  |  |  |  |  |  |  |  |  |
| 67 | Treiorwg Organic Farm |  |  |  |  | ♦ | ♦ |  |  |  |  |  |  |  |  |  | ♦ |
| 68 | Trigonos Centre | ♦ |  |  | ♦ |  | ♦ | ♦ | ♦ |  |  | ♦ |  |  |  |  | ♦ |
| 70 | Wilderness Trust |  |  |  |  |  | ♦ |  | ♦ |  |  |  |  |  |  |  | ♦ |
| | **South West England** | | | | | | | | | | | | | | | | |
| 101 | Ashburton Centre |  |  | ♦ | ♦ |  |  | ♦ |  | ♦ | ♦ |  |  |  | ♦ |  | ♦ |
| 74 | Acorn Centre |  |  | ♦ | ♦ |  |  |  |  |  | ♦ |  |  |  |  |  |  |
| 75 | Beacon Centre |  | ♦ | ♦ | ♦ |  |  |  |  | ♦ | ♦ | ♦ | ♦ | ♦ | ♦ |  | ♦ |
| 77 | CAER |  |  | ♦ | ♦ |  | ♦ |  |  | ♦ | ♦ | ♦ | ♦ | ♦ | ♦ |  | ♦ |
| 80 | Grimstone |  | ♦ | ♦ | ♦ |  |  |  |  |  | ♦ |  |  |  | ♦ |  |  |
| 80 | Hawkwood | ♦ | ♦ | ♦ | ♦ | ♦ | ♦ |  |  |  | ♦ | ♦ |  |  |  |  | ♦ |
| 82 | Hazelwood | ♦ | ♦ |  |  |  |  |  |  |  |  |  |  |  |  |  |  |
| 83 | Lower Shaw Farm |  |  |  |  |  |  | ♦ |  |  |  |  |  |  |  |  |  |
| 84 | Magdalen Farm | ♦ | ♦ |  |  |  | ♦ |  | ♦ |  | ♦ | ♦ |  |  | ♦ |  | ♦ |
| 86 | Monkton Wyld | ♦ | ♦ | ♦ |  |  |  |  |  |  |  | ♦ | ♦ |  |  |  | ♦ |
| 87 | Old Boswednack Farm |  | ♦ |  |  |  |  |  |  | ♦ |  |  |  | ♦ |  |  |  |
| 88 | Holton Lee | ♦ | ♦ | ♦ | ♦ | ♦ | ♦ |  |  | ♦ | ♦ |  |  |  | ♦ | ♦ | ♦ |
| 89 | Pelican Centre | ♦ | ♦ |  |  |  | ♦ |  |  | ♦ | ♦ |  |  |  | ♦ |  |  |

| | 91 | 92 | 93 | 94 | 96 | 99 | 100 | 105 | 105 | 106 | 108 | 108 | 109 | 110 | 111 | 111 | 112 | 113 | 114 | 115 |
|---|---|---|---|---|---|---|---|---|---|---|---|---|---|---|---|---|---|---|---|---|
| | ◆ | ◆ | ◆ | | | ◆ | | | | | | ◆ | | | | | ◆ | | | |
| | | | ◆ | ◆ | | | | | | | ◆ | | | | ◆ | | ◆ | ◆ | | |
| | | ◆ | ◆ | | | | | | ◆ | | | ◆ | ◆ | | | ◆ | | | ◆ | ◆ |
| | | ◆ | ◆ | ◆ | | | | | ◆ | | | ◆ | ◆ | | | ◆ | | | ◆ | ◆ |
| | | | | | | | | | | | | | | | | | | | | |
| | | | ◆ | | | | | ◆ | | | ◆ | ◆ | | | ◆ | | | | | |
| | ◆ | ◆ | ◆ | | | | | ◆ | ◆ | | ◆ | ◆ | | | ◆ | | | | | ◆ |
| | ◆ | ◆ | ◆ | ◆ | | | | ◆ | | | ◆ | ◆ | ◆ | | ◆ | | | | ◆ | |
| | | | | | | ◆ | | | | | | | | | | | ◆ | ◆ | | |
| | | | | | | ◆ | | | | | | ◆ | | | | | ◆ | ◆ | | |
| | | | | | | ◆ | | ◆ | | ◆ | | | | | | | ◆ | | | |
| | | | | | | | ◆ | | | | | | | | | | ◆ | | | |
| | | ◆ | ◆ | | ◆ | | ◆ | | ◆ | | | ◆ | ◆ | | | | ◆ | | | |
| | | ◆ | ◆ | | | | | ◆ | | ◆ | | ◆ | | | | | | | | |
| | | ◆ | ◆ | | | | | ◆ | | | ◆ | | ◆ | | | | | | | |
| | | | | ◆ | | | | ◆ | | ◆ | ◆ | | | | | | | | | ◆ |

**Places**

- 91 Schumacher College
- 92 Self Realization Centre
- 93 Shambhala
- 94 Sheldon Centre
- 96 Tordown
- 99 Yarner Trust
- 100 Yeo Cottage

**South East England**

- 105 Braziers
- 105 Cherwell Centre
- 106 Commonwork
- 108 Emerson College
- 108 Equilibrium
- 109 Four Winds
- 110 The Friars
- 111 Little Grove
- 111 Old Alresford
- 112 Redfield Centre
- 113 Sedlescombe Vineyard
- 114 Stacklands
- 115 Turvey Abbey

# Workshop Seeker's Index

| page | Venue | S1 | S2 | S3 | S4 | S5 | S6 | S7 | S8 | S9 | S10 | S11 | S12 | S13 | S14 | S15 | work | acc |
|---|---|---|---|---|---|---|---|---|---|---|---|---|---|---|---|---|---|---|
| | **Greater London** | | | | | | | | | | | | | | | | | |
| 120 | Grail Centre | | | | | | | | | | | | | | | | | |
| 121 | Marie Reparatrice | | | | | | | | | | | | | | ◆ | ◆ | | |
| 122 | Ruth White Centre | | | ◆ | ◆ | | | | | | | | | | | | | |
| 123 | St Michael's Convent | ◆ | ◆ | ◆ | ◆ | | | | | ◆ | | | | | ◆ | ◆ | | |
| | **Outside the UK** | | | | | | | | | | | | | | | | | |
| 126 | Beau Champ | ◆ | | | | | ◆ | ◆ | ◆ | | | | | | | | ◆ | |
| 127 | Le Blé en Herbe | | ◆ | ◆ | ◆ | | | ◆ | ◆ | | | ◆ | | | | | ◆ | |
| 128 | Coat-Aillis | | | ◆ | ◆ | | | | | | | | | | | | | |
| 130 | Holiday Azogires | ◆ | | | | ◆ | | | | | ◆ | | | | | | | |
| 131 | Skyros - Atsitsa | ◆ | ◆ | ◆ | ◆ | ◆ | ◆ | | ◆ | ◆ | ◆ | ◆ | | | ◆ | | ◆ | ◆ |
| 132 | Chrysalis | | | ◆ | ◆ | | | | | ◆ | ◆ | ◆ | | | ◆ | | | |
| 133 | Az Agr Montali | | | | | | | ◆ | | | | | | | | | | |
| 134 | Cortijo Romero | | ◆ | ◆ | ◆ | | | ◆ | | ◆ | ◆ | ◆ | ◆ | | ◆ | | | ◆ |
| 136 | Sunseed | | | | | | | | | | | | | | | | ◆ | |
| 137 | Huzur Vadisi | ◆ | ◆ | ◆ | | | | | | | | | | | ◆ | | | |

# The Alphabetical Index

## Alphabetical Index

Dear Reader, We hope that you have found this edition of **Places to BE** to be both useful and enjoyable. We welcome your feedback and invite you to fill out this postcard and return it to us.

**Please tick one or both**

❏ I run/organise workshops/courses    ❏ I participate in workshops/courses

**What are you looking for most from a directory like this?**
**Please score (I = first)**

☐ individual retreats    ☐ group retreats    ☐ venues to hire

☐ led workshops    ☐ "alternative" B&Bs    ☐ working holidays

☐ ...........................    ☐ ...........................    ☐ ...........................

☐ **Please tick if you use electronic mail or other Internet services**

**What features would you add to a future edition?**


**How did you hear about Places to BE?**

**Name**

**Address**


**Postcode**

❏ We will continue to mail you about this and other publications distributed by *Edge of Time* unless you tick this box

- - - - - - - - - - - - - - - - - - - - - - - - - - - - - - - - - - - - - - - - - - - - - - - - - - - - - -

Do you run or do you know of a venue not listed in this edition of **Places to BE**? Make sure that we know about that venue when we come to compile **Places to BE 1999/2000**.
Fill out this postcard and return it to us. Don't forget the stamp.

**Name of venue**


**Address**


**Postcode**


**Telephone number**


**Fax number**


**Electronic Mail**


**Contact Name**


**How did you hear about Places to BE?**

**Coherent Visions**
**BCM Visions**
**London**
**WC1N 3XX**

**Coherent Visions**
**BCM Visions**
**London**
**WC1N 3XX**